W9-BRB-486

Wide Views
and a
Loving Heart

*The Life and Ministry
of Bishop Levi Scott*

Joseph F. DiPaolo

*Published by the Historical Society of the
Eastern Pennsylvania Conference of
The United Methodist Church*

Wide Views and a Loving Heart
The Life and Ministry of Bishop Levi Scott

Published by the Historical Society of the Eastern Pennsylvania
Conference of The United Methodist Church
St. George's United Methodist Church
326 New Street
Philadelphia, Pennsylvania, 19106

Copyright © 2018 by Joseph F. DiPaolo

All rights reserved. No part of this publication may be reproduced,
stored in retrieval system, or transmitted to any form or by any
means – electronic, mechanical, photocopy, recording, or any other
– except for brief quotations in printed reviews, without the prior
permission of the author.

Cover: Pencil drawing of Levi Scott by Delaware artist David
Chalfont (1865-1931), late nineteenth century (*Eastern
Pennsylvania Conference Historical Society*).

Cover Design by Mark Stoner of Lancaster, Pennsylvania

Printed in the United States of America

ISBN 978-1-5323-8610-7

To Christina, Laura and Timothy,
of whom I am immensely proud.

Table of Contents

Portrait of Bishop Levi Scott (late 19th century)
by Jefferson David Chalfont (1856-1931)
(Barratt's Chapel and Museum, Frederica, Delaware).

Foreword

In May of 2015 I was researching African American life in early nineteenth century southern New Castle County, Delaware. I noticed a peculiar occurrence as an intriguing figure began to emerge. The person who materialized was a major contributor to African American church life throughout the Delmarva Peninsula, the Methodist Episcopal Church and beyond. The sleeping giant of history who was hiding in plain sight was Bishop Levi Scott.

As I dug into the material, the trail led to Lee-Haven United Methodist Church in Townsend, Delaware. Originally known as Lee Chapel, it is the oldest locally recognized African American congregation. Combing through local histories and Lee Chapel's organizing documents and records, I quickly discovered that the white-controlled Methodist Episcopal Church was the dominant church for African American church membership in early nineteenth century Delaware. Within this history I was astonished to learn about the highly unusual story of Levi Scott. Young Levi was a local white farm boy who experienced his Christian conversion at a prayer meeting conducted by women in the home of a free African American family who were leading members of Lee Chapel, the forerunner of Lee-Haven UMC.

I was intrigued. I wanted to learn more about Levi Scott, so I headed to Barratt's Chapel which houses the archives of the United Methodist Church in Delaware. While at Barratt's, the curator, understanding the unique nature of my research project, asked if I knew of Rev. Joseph DiPaolo and his work on Bishop Scott. After the introductions were made, Rev. DiPaolo and I began exchanging emails, phone calls and comparing research notes. I quickly realized that he was engaged in an extensive, nationwide research effort, systematically scouring archives near and far for papers of the bishop that had been locked away for generations.

The Akan people of Ghana, West Africa have a belief that "it is not taboo to fetch what is at risk of being left behind." This belief, called Sankofa, emphasizes the wisdom of learning from events of the past to ensure a strong future. In Rev. DiPaolo's *Wide Views and a Loving Heart, The Life and Ministry of Bishop Levi Scott,* my hope is that current and future generations will learn of Bishop Scott and his wise leadership, using it as a timeless guide for serving and living.

Bishop Levi Scott's influence in the Methodist Episcopal Church stands tallest during the tumultuous days leading up to our nation's Civil War. Rev. DiPaolo carefully navigates us through the growing challenges in the bishop's ecclesiastical life, which mirror the growing tensions of a fractured nation. In this time-frame, we see the skill with which Scott dares to build bridges between clergy and church leaders, as growing factions attempt to further split an already divided church. Scott goes on to be among the most respected and influential bishops of the Methodist Episcopal Church.

The lesson I personally find most enduring in Bishop Scott's life is his courage to participate in cross cultural ministry. Scott's example of sharing the gospel of Jesus Christ while worshiping and working with culturally different communities is a powerful example for twenty-first century Christians as we struggle with the issues of diversity and pluralism.

Bishop Scott's life teaches us the value of advocating for the rights of people who are outside the mainstream. He lived his beliefs, he spoke up for those who were voiceless in the halls of power and who had no seat at the decision-making table. During his ministry, Bishops Scott accomplished more to benefit the lives of Africans and African Americans than most white clergy of his era would have dared to venture. He set in motion institutionally important initiatives that people of African descent could not have accomplished through their own agency at that racially divisive moment in our history.

In the life of our nation and in our faith communities we are, again, feeling the tensions of division, with "all or none" and "either/or" resolutions to consequential questions of humanity in our daily lives. Collectively, we have failed to model God's love in the world and we find ourselves on the brink of splitting as a church and retreating to our separate corners. Bishop Levi Scott models bridge-building in a way that can benefit the present-day church.

I for one am most grateful that Rev. Joseph DiPaolo has decided at this auspicious time "to fetch what is at risk of being left behind," and to bring the story of Bishop Scott's life forward for us to ponder in the twenty-first century. Rev. DiPaolo offers us a treasure in the significant stories of Bishop Scott's life – valued lessons, fruitful for our present age, and for ages to come.

Love, Peace and Sankofa
Anthony B. Johnson, member
Commission on Archives and History
Peninsula Delaware Annual Conference
The United Methodist Church

Introduction

In 1901, Delaware Supreme Court Chief Justice Charles B. Lore delivered an address on the history of Odessa, relating stories and events stretching back more than two hundred years. More than half his lecture, however, focused on the life and legacy of Odessa native Levi Scott, whom Lore knew personally, and who had served as a Methodist bishop for thirty years. Citing Scott's "spotless name and... life of singular purity and power," Lore concluded his sketch by saying, "I regard Levi Scott as one of the greatest men this peninsula has produced, measuring him by all the rules of elemental manhood."[1]

Though largely forgotten today, Levi Scott was well-known and widely respected in his day. He played a prominent role in shaping the Methodism of the nineteenth century, especially as it struggled with the status and empowerment of African Americans. Scott was the first Methodist bishop to ordain black preachers as deacons and elders who enjoyed full membership in an annual conference, which he did in Liberia in 1853. Bishop Scott was instrumental in creating the office of missionary bishop, and in the appointment of the first black bishop in the Methodist Episcopal (ME) Church. He was the first bishop to preside over an official conference of African American preachers, in 1857, and played an important role in founding the Delaware and Washington Conferences, in which African Americans enjoyed full clergy status for the first time in the ME Church within in the United States.

Scott's unlikely origins render all the more extraordinary his rise to national leadership. A farm boy with little formal education, Scott became self-educated in literature, history, theology, and classical languages. He developed into an eloquent and able writer and speaker, and advanced so far as to serve as a teacher, college administrator and book editor. He was the first Methodist bishop whose father had been a Methodist minister, and the first bishop who hailed from the state of Delaware. Scott spent the last twenty years of his life living on the farm where he had been raised as a boy, and was regarded by neighbors, friends, and colleagues as a man of sound judgment and saintly character.

Levi Scott deserves a larger place in the collective memory of Delawareans and Methodists alike.

I am grateful to friends, scholars and librarians, too many to name, who assisted me in the research and preparation of this book. I am especially appreciative to Rev. Phil Lawton and Barb Duffin, Historian and Archivist, respectively, at Barratt's Chapel in Frederica, Delaware. It was at their request that I began researching Levi Scott's life, in order to present a paper for a gathering of United Methodist historians in Delaware in 2016. They also offered invaluable assistance in providing me with access to the collection at Barratt's Chapel.

Similar roles were played by Donna Miller, archivist at Old St. George's in Philadelphia, Rob Shindle, archivist at Lovely Lane Museum and Library in Baltimore, and the fine staff at the General Commission on Archives and History (GCAH) of The United Methodist Church in Madison, New Jersey, especially Mark Shenise and Dale Patterson.

Two fine scholars, Dr. Eric Cheezum and Dr. Ian Straker, offered important suggestions and corrections to my framing of Scott's story amid the controversy over slavery. Finally, and not least, I am grateful to Anthony Johnson, who supplied me with invaluable research leads, as well as insight into the life of both the free and enslaved people of Delaware in the 19th century. He took time from his business on several occasions to shepherd me around the Odessa area to become familiar with the lay of the land which Levi Scott knew so well. In Anthony, I obtained an added blessing from this project: a new friend.

Joseph F. DiPaolo
Wayne, Pennsylvania
September 2018

Portrait of Levi Scott as a young man
(Barratt's Chapel and Museum, Frederica, Delaware).

Anne Scott's Boy

Levi Scott was born October 11, 1802 on his family's farm near Odessa, Delaware, then known as Cantwell Bridge. The town took its name from a toll bridge built in the 1730s over the Appoquinimink River by Richard Cantwell, and became a well-known stopping place for travelers between the Chesapeake Bay and the Delaware River. Though only a few dozen families lived in the village itself, Cantwell Bridge was a hub for the shipment of farm products and other goods to markets in Wilmington, Philadelphia, Baltimore and Annapolis. Among the thriving local businesses at the turn of the nineteenth century was a large tannery owned by William Corbit, and a furniture shop owned by cabinet maker (and Levi's relative) John Janvier.

Levi, however, would spend most of his childhood living and working on the family farm with his widowed mother and two brothers. Levi was the youngest of three children born to Thomas and Anne Scott, but his mother had been married once before. In 1791, Anne March had married John Lattomus, who owned a farm along the Appoquinimink. He died in 1793, after fathering two children, Diana, who died as a young child, and John, with whom Levi was close growing up. "I loved him," Scott later wrote of his stepbrother, "and he had an almost boundless influence over me." In 1796, Anne remarried to Thomas Scott, who took charge of the farm, and the couple went on to have three children: Sarah, who died as a child, Thomas, and Levi.[1]

In addition to running his farm, Thomas Scott was an active member of the Methodist Episcopal Church, serving as class leader and local preacher. Levi described his father as "a deeply pious and devoted man, a good, earnest and useful preacher," but not from personal memory. Hearing a call to full-time ministry, Thomas Scott joined the Philadelphia Conference in the spring of 1803 as an itinerant preacher and assigned to serve the Queen Anne Circuit on Maryland's Eastern Shore. His ministry, however, was short. When Levi was just eight months old, Thomas Scott took ill and died, barely a month into his first appointment, and was buried in Centreville, Maryland.[2]

Anne had traveled from the farm to the bedside of her dying husband, who bestowed a final blessing upon his infant son. Levi wrote that, after the funeral, "my bereaved and heart-stricken mother set her sorrowful face toward her once cheerful and happy but now desolate home." Twice widowed, Anne found herself left with three young sons to raise, along with a farm encumbered with debt. A determined and talented woman, she resolved to retain the farm and keep her family together on it, which eventually included her sisters, Araminta and Sarah. In time, Anne's capable management cleared the land of debt, and even enlarged it with additional acreage. The homestead would remain in the family for decades thereafter, and later became the home of Levi and his family during his final years.

Growing up, Levi Scott was happy, energetic and popular among his peers; by his own words, "buoyant in spirit ...[and] fond of fun and frolic." He also evinced a talent for music and took up the violin. He became quite proficient, and was "in much request at the social gatherings of his young friends... playing the fiddle for dancing parties at quiltings, corn-huskings, and weddings." In this period, most Methodists were suspicious

A VIEW AT *APPOQUINIMINK*, STATE of DELAWARE.

An image of Odessa, then called Cantwell Bridge, dated 1805-1820, drawn by G.W. Janvier (*Historic Odessa Foundation*).

----

of instrumental music, and the violin in particular, concerned that it enticed people to sin. Early 19th century Methodist conversion stories not infrequently include a somber account of a new believer giving up or even smashing his fiddle. So it would be with Scott, though later he would return to the instrument.[3]

It was Methodism that would profoundly shape Levi Scott and set the course of his life and career. At the time of Levi's birth, there was no Methodist congregation in Odessa. The nearest one met in a frame chapel, five miles to the south, called Union Meeting House. This was the Scott family church, and it was here that young Levi was taught the Christian faith and trained in the ways of the Lord. Levi revered the influence of the father he did not remember, and credited receiving Thomas' dying blessing as a baby with "the gracious influences of the Holy Spirit, which have accompanied me all through life."[4] Like St. Augustine, however, the principal spiritual influence on Scott's life was his mother.

Methodism in Delaware

Methodism began as a revival movement in eighteenth-century England under the leadership of John Wesley (1703-1791) and his brother Charles (1707-1788). In the early days, Methodism was not a church, but a renewal movement within the Anglican Church, its early congregations called "societies," rather than churches. The first enduring societies in America began in the 1760s in Maryland, New York, and Pennsylvania. With the collapse of Anglicanism in America after the Revolution, Methodists organized themselves as a church in 1784, calling the new denomination the Methodist Episcopal (ME) Church.

It was not easy to avoid Methodist revivalism in Delaware and on the Eastern Shore during the period in which Levi grew up, despite the loss of his preacher-father. A frequent stomping ground of Francis Asbury, Freeborn Garrettson and other famous early itinerants, the Delmarva Peninsula was home to thirty-one percent of the membership of the ME Church in 1784, the year of its founding. While that percentage declined as the church expanded throughout the nation, Methodism became the dominant spiritual force in the region. By 1820, nearly twenty percent of the adult population of Delmarva were members of the Methodist Episcopal Church.[5]

Methodism's influence went even beyond what that statistic suggests, since it was not uncommon in those days of high membership standards for attendance to exceed membership. In addition, the Methodists were aggressive evangelists, especially through the agency of camp meetings – large, outdoor evangelistic gatherings that brought people together from miles around for a week or more to hear the emotive preaching of a host of ministers. Pioneer Bishop Francis Asbury called camp meetings "fishing with a big net." In rural areas, such as New Castle County, Delaware, these encampments also served an important social function, attracting a mix of believers, seekers, merchants and young rowdies looking for mischief. Levi Scott attended camp meetings as a child, tried to disrupt them as a youth, and preached at them as a minister.

An image of the home where Levi Scott was born, from an
article that appeared in the October 9, 1902 *Christian Advocate.*

Years later, Levi's friend and ministerial colleague, J. B.
McCullough, remembered Anne Scott as a "devoted Methodist...
of the primitive type." McCullough described Anne's "semi-
Quaker costume, and her thrilling shouts of praise in the class-
meeting which, in the little rural church, preceded the Sabbath
morning sermon in those days." Thirty five years after her death,
a clergy member of the Wilmington Conference wrote that,
among the older people of the Odessa area, "'Mother Scott' is
spoken of with nearly as much reverence as the Bishop himself."[6]
Bishop Scott himself credited his faith to "the strong religious
training to which, from infancy, I was subjected by my own
sainted mother." The bishop later wrote of a nightly ritual before
bed, which consisted of Anne leading her boys in the singing of a
hymn, praying with them, and then having them recite the
Lord's Prayer. And Sunday worship was non-negotiable:

> ...she took us regularly to meeting, at the old Union Meeting-
> house, on Sabbath morning, and required us to read portions
> of the Bible to her in the afternoon and evening. Scarcely any
> state of the weather could keep her from the house of God.
> How certain and familiar that sound on Sabbath morning:
> "Come boys and put the horse to the carriage and let us go to
> meeting."[7]

As a youth, however, Levi rebelled against the faith of his parents, and "severely tried" his mother's faith and patience. "After I left the maternal roof and went to learn a trade, [I] became associated with wild and wicked youths," he wrote, "and I lost, to a great extent, my religious impressions and thought-fulness, and became careless and disorderly in my conduct." There are hints Scott was a bit more rowdy as a youth than his Victorian biographers wanted to reveal. His friend, Rev. J. B. McCullough, reported that, before his conversion, Scott "was as profuse and original in his use of profanity as Andrew Jackson... [which] was saying a great deal." Scott also enjoyed going to Methodist camp meetings with other local youths, to mock the participants and disrupt the meetings. Writing about one he attended while inwardly struggling with God's call to faith, Scott wrote that he was led "to behave worse at that camp meeting than I had ever done before."[8]

Conversion Experience and Call

In his sixteenth year, Levi moved to Georgetown,[9] to begin an apprenticeship as a carpenter, but returned home after just a few months, due to illness and unhappiness with his situation. He renewed an apprenticeship locally with a cousin named John Janvier, who was a cabinetmaker. It was in 1822, while still training under Janvier, and just a few days after his twentieth birthday, that Levi "came home" to the faith of his father and mother. His story has all the classic elements of an early nineteenth century Methodist conversion narrative: an "awakening" under powerful preaching to his sinfulness and need for redemption; followed by a period of struggle and anguished seeking of salvation; and finally, the moment of breakthrough, resulting in peace with God, followed by ecstatic joy, the pursuit of holiness, and a passion to bear witness to others. Scott's story, however, has a few interesting twists to it.

For one, his awakening occurred under Presbyterian auspices. Sometime in late 1821 or early 1822, a Presbyterian preacher named Ogden came to town to hold a weeknight preaching service at the local schoolhouse. The visiting preacher was put up at the Scott family homestead. Levi was employed as

"Old Union," Scott's home church as a boy and again in later life. The congregation dates at least to 1789, when Joseph Dickinson deeded land to a board of trustees, who built a log meeting house on the site called Dickinson's Chapel. This was rebuilt in 1798 as a frame chapel, and was the church Levi Scott knew as a boy. Francis Asbury preached at Union on March 23, 1810, and young Levi may have heard the bishop preach that day. In 1847, the frame church was replaced by the structure above, which still stands today. The obelisk marks Bishop Scott's grave. Services discontinued in the early 1900s; the property is maintained today by the Old Union Church Society[10] *(Old Union Church Society).*

----

the sexton for the evening, getting the building in order for the service, and cleaning up after. He heard Rev. Ogden preach on Acts 24:25, the story of Felix's procrastination in responding to the gospel. Scott later recalled, "The preacher swept away all the refuge of lies in which sinners trust, and made me feel that I had not one solid and reasonable excuse for postponing the work of salvation another hour." That night, Scott bowed in his room, and for the first time in years, "tried to pray." But no peace came. For months he was haunted by "gloomy thoughts," convinced he was lost, and that he might "drop into hell while asleep."[11]

It was only after the conversion of his brother, John Lattomus, that Scott thought there might be hope for him. Levi later wrote that his stepbrother had been "light-hearted, full of good humor and mischief," and showed no interest in the things of God. But at a summer camp meeting in 1822, John came to faith in Christ, and his example motivated Levi. "Brother John is converted," he thought, "and now the way is clear."[12]

Levi now began an earnest pursuit of saving faith. He read his Bible, gave up sinful habits (including his violin, substituting the more acceptable German flute), and attended services, but for months did not find peace. When that moment came, it would provide the second twist in the story. On the night of October 16, 1822, he attended a prayer meeting at the home of Isaac and Betsy Carter, a free black couple who lived about two miles from Scott's home, in the neighborhood called Fieldsborough. While Methodism was rapidly segregating at this time, it was still not unknown for blacks and whites to worship together and even hold integrated class meetings. Betsy and Isaac were property owners, members of Union Church, and later, charter members of Lee Chapel ME Church, a black congregation in Blackbird. Isaac was recalled as "one of the sweet singers of our Methodist Israel," though it appears that Betsy had charge of the meeting Levi attended. "This prayer meeting was conducted by Christian ladies," Scott recalled. "They gathered around me, and sung and prayed, and counseled me." Soon, the breakthrough came. After visualizing the story of the woman who touched the hem of Jesus' robe and found healing, he imagined himself reaching out to do the same:

> In the twinkle of an eye my burden was gone, my cry of agony was hushed... O it was an ecstatic moment! I seemed flying through the midst of heaven, my body and my clothing as white as the driven snow, and angel bands around me, gently touching me, and singing as I had never heard before. It was not of long duration. I came to myself, and the people seemed the most beautiful and the most happy I had ever seen.[13]

Scott often spoke of that night in later years as his spiritual birthday. He reported that when he told his mother of his conversion, she jumped and danced around the house, which surprised him. "[This was] the only time I remember her to have jumped," he wrote," for she was quite steady and faithful, and seldom made much ado about anything."[14]

An image of a home prayer meeting led by African Americans, from later in the 19th century. Levi Scott was converted at a prayer meeting led by black women (*Library of Congress*).

As his colleague John A. Roche later put it, Scott had "a good Presbyterian conviction... [and] a grand Methodist conversion – a most happy combination."[15] With all the zeal typical of a new convert, Scott now immersed himself in the faith, becoming a member of Union Church, and also the class-meeting in Fieldsborough. Methodist services began soon after in Odessa as well, which may be the earliest root of today's St. Paul's United Methodist Church. Scott soon rose to leadership, and sensed a call to preach, saying, "My heart was stirred to call sinners to repentance." In August 1823, he received his exhorter's license, and in February 1825, his local preacher's license.[16]

Scott's conversion sparked an intellectual awakening. Growing up on a farm that did not use slave labor, it fell upon Levi and his brothers to do the bulk of the daily work to maintain it. In the spring, summer and fall, farm work consumed his time, and only during the winters did he attend school, resulting in an education which was, he said, "very limited." Though he could read, write, and do basic math, he later said, "I knew nothing of grammar, philosophy, geography, or of history." Though his lack of formal education was by no

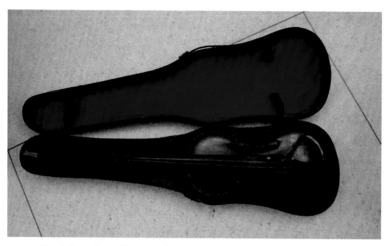

Levi Scott's violin, in the museum of Barratt's Chapel.
Bishop Scott is said to have made the instrument himself.

----

means unusual among Methodist preachers during this era, it deeply embarrassed Levi, and he determined to apply himself to learning. "Now I was all athirst for God," he wrote, "and at the same time, all athirst for mental improvement."[7]

He borrowed books, which he propped up over his work bench while on the job, and progressed so rapidly that within three years he took a job as a private tutor with a prominent local family named Naudain. Arnold Naudain lived with his wife Jemima and their children in a home that still stands off today's Route 896. A "self-educated, intelligent and scientific farmer," Naudain was also a Methodist lay preacher, and was evidently impressed when he heard Levi deliver his first sermon in the Salem Methodist Protestant Church in Blackbird in 1825.[18]

A few years later, when living in Philadelphia as a circuit preacher, Scott took on formalized studies in Latin and Greek. Still later, he would serve three years as a teacher and administrator for the preparatory school associated with Dickinson College, in Carlisle, Pennsylvania. He also would receive two honorary degrees, a Master of Arts (MA) from Wesleyan University in 1840, and a Doctor of Divinity (DD) from Delaware College in 1846. J. B McCullough later called Scott "one of the best self-educated men we have ever known."[19]

Levi's Tribute to his Mother

Anne Scott was a leading member of the Union congregation, and became a founder and matriarch of St. Paul's Church in Odessa, when it was established in the 1830s. After her death, Levi Scott wrote a short obituary for his mother, which appeared in the Christian Advocate, *the denominational paper published in New York, in its October 11, 1848 issue.*

August 20 [1848] – near Cantwell's Bridge, Del., Mrs. Anne Scott in, I think, her 84th year. My father, Thomas Scott, who was received into the Philadelphia Conference as a probationer in the spring of 1803, died in the following June. At his death, the charge of a small farm, then considerably in debt, and of a family of three small children, of whom the writer, then an infant, was the youngest, devolved on my mother. By her energy and perseverance, the farm was freed from debt and enlarged, and her children raised in a style of respectability equal to her limited means. When she joined the ME Church, I do not know, it being at a period beyond my earliest recollections. She was a uniform, faithful member, [and] always, when not providentially prevented, in her placed at public service and at class. She always, too, had worship in the family, which, until her children were prepared by age and grace to take her place, she conducted herself; and never will her earnest, fervent prayers be forgotten! Constitutionally modest, she never made a high profession of religion. But her cheerful, uniform devotedness to God, under all circumstances, was her witness that she enjoyed a sweet and steady communion with him. Her end was peace. In March last, she was attacked with vertigo, and fell, and fractured her hip. After months of helplessness and deep suffering, which she bore with remarkable patience and holy cheerfulness, she sunk, without a struggle or a groan, into the arms of her Saviour, and found her long-sought rest.

L. Scott

A Methodist Circuit Rider, from *Harper's Weekly* in 1867. As the
country expanded during the 19th century, circuit riders were
renowned for following the wagon tracks to new settlements to
plant churches. By 1850, Methodists accounted for more than thirty
four percent of all church members, outnumbering by two-to-one
Presbyterians, Congregationalists and Episcopalians put together.
A saying among frontier settlements on stormy days was
"Nothing out today but crows and Methodist preachers."

2

Circuit Riding Preacher

On January 28, 1826, Levi rode to Smyrna, Delaware for an event that would forever change the course of his life. He was headed to Asbury ME Church for the quarterly conference meeting of the Smyrna Circuit. The original purpose of quarterly conference was that of a business meeting, as representatives from all the churches on the circuit dealt with financial, membership and property concerns. By the late eighteenth century, however, these quarterly meetings had evolved into great celebrations, marked by special preaching services, love feasts (a highly participatory service of hymn-singing, testimony and prayer), and the celebration of communion and baptism. One early itinerant described these great gatherings:

> Methodists would go forty and fifty miles to quarterly meetings. These were our great festivals. Here we renewed our covenants with God and his people, obtained encouragement and strength in our souls, and rejoiced together in the salvation of God.[1]

Among the matters of business to be handled in this spiritually charged atmosphere was the consideration of young men who had been proposed for ordained ministry. It was for this purpose that Levi Scott came to Smyrna. With the backing of Presiding Elder Jacob Moore, and the enthusiastic support of Union Church, Levi Scott was approved, and recommended to the Philadelphia Conference. Less than two months later, that body met for its annual session in Philadelphia. "I was not there," Scott recalled years later. "Full of painful doubt as to whether it was the will of God that I should become a traveling preacher, I remained at home making provisional arrangements should I be received."[2]

He was, and found himself assigned to the Talbot Circuit on Maryland's Eastern Shore. As a colleague later described it, Talbot Circuit "embraced a wide district... [with] preaching twice or thrice every Sabbath, and on each week day, for three out of every four weeks." Despite the demanding schedule, Scott clearly enjoyed his work. Many years later, long after he had moved into administrative roles in the larger church, Scott often was heard to say, "The happiest days of my ministry were when I was on a circuit."[3] In a letter sent to his brother John Lattomus in January 1827, Scott seemed in high spirits, relating anecdotes, and his enthusiasm for his work:

> Our societies generally appear in a good state. In Easton we
> have a more encouraging prospect than we have had during
> the year. The members appear to be hungering and thirsting
> after righteousness. Yes, and many are filled. Glory, glory be
> to God.[4]

Methodist circuit riders were constantly on the move, traveling on horseback to any number of congregations linked together on a circuit. "The average circuit in those days was from twelve to twenty appointments," noted Scott's biographer. "Many of the preaching places were in private homes, usually at the home in which the society held its class-meeting."[5] It was arduous work. An 1855 study of 672 early circuit riders by Methodist historian Abel Stevens found that fifty-seven percent of them lasted less than twelve years on the job. Nearly half were dead by age thirty; sixty percent were dead by age forty.[6]

Barratt's Chapel, in Federica, Delaware, built in 1780. In 1784 Francis Asbury and Thomas Coke met here to plan the founding of the Methodist Episcopal Church, which occurred at the famous Christmas Conference later that year in Baltimore. Levi Scott preached here as a young minister while assigned to the Dover Circuit, 1827-1828.

Scott preached multiple times each week, met with small accountability groups (class meetings), baptized children and adults, married couples, buried the dead, and preached at summer camp meetings. His training for ministry followed the usual pattern of that day. He was received "on trial," where he learned his craft on the job, under the supervision of more experienced ministers. The first, on Talbot Circuit in 1826, was 65-year old Charles Reed, a native of New Jersey, who had been ordained by Bishop Francis Asbury. Of Reed's ministry it was remembered, "[t]he love of God manifest in the gift of his Son for the salvation of a lost and ruined world, and the atonement made by Jesus Christ, were the themes on which he chiefly delighted to converse and preach."[7] The second, on Dover Circuit in 1827, was Rev. James Bateman, remembered as "a genius in his day, and a truly original preacher."[8]

While in his ministerial apprenticeship, Scott also kept up with assigned studies, on which he was tested at the ensuing annual conference session. In 1828, he was admitted into full conference membership and ordained a deacon by Bishop Enoch George. That same year, Scott was assigned for the first time to a city charge, in Philadelphia, as one of a team of four ministers serving a circuit that included St. George's, Ebenezer, Salem, Nazareth, and the only black ME Church in the city, Zoar. The charge included 2,664 white and 305 black members, and was centered at St. George's, the oldest Methodist church in the region, dating to 1769. As recalled by Rev. Anthony Atwood, (who would become Scott's colleague there in 1829), St. George's "was filled at every service, and for a generation after, upstairs and down. The ministers preached three times each Sabbath, and one evening in the week."[9]

In charge of the circuit in 1828 was Rev. Samuel Doughty, just six years older than Scott, but already a popular preacher and rising star, who had published several sermons in the *Methodist Magazine*. Doughty died suddenly, however, in the fall of 1828, and the leadership of the circuit fell to the other experienced preacher on the charge, Jacob Gruber. Famously eccentric, Gruber had come to national prominence a decade earlier when he was arrested for inciting slaves to insurrection, after preaching against slavery before a mixed crowd of blacks and whites in Maryland.[10] The fourth minister was Thomas J. Thompson, a fellow novice with whom Scott formed a deep and life-long friendship. In 1829, Scott was reappointed to the St. George's Circuit, which was now led by Rev. Manning Force. Before retiring, Force would serve six terms as a presiding elder, and was remembered years later as "emphatically the friend and counselor of young preachers."[11]

St. George's was then "the central locality where our people gathered," recalled Atwood, and frequently hosted the Philadelphia Conference's annual meeting, including the 1828 session, when Scott was ordained a deacon. When conference was in session, lay members from around the region came for services which were held every day. The crowds were even larger on the Sunday that fell during the annual meeting. "The Sabbath was usually a high day," Atwood wrote. "The bishop holding the

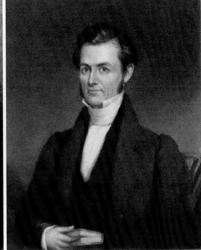

Left: Rev. Manning Force, who had charge of St. George's Circuit, 1829-1830. Right: Rev. Anthony Atwood, who was assigned there alongside Scott in 1829; the two became lifelong friends.

----

the conference was expected to preach and ordain either the elders or the deacons in that church. And this ordination service was deemed, especially by persons from the country, a great sight." Atwood went on to describe the fervor and excitement which must have impressed the young Levi Scott, who had been raised in rural Delaware:

> From ten to thirty ministers were certain to occupy the pulpit, the chancel, and the northern corner seats. In the opposite corner sat the most elegant and dignified ladies that ever graced a place of worship... A conference room was built on New Street, where business could proceed regularly while public worship could be continued three times each day in the church, less than a rod distant. Public worship all day was deemed a necessity, because of the many leading families coming in from the country to attend the conference. It had as much interest with our people at that time as the great feasts of the Jews had with that ancient people long ago. What the families heard, saw and felt in conference week served as matters of conversation for the

balance of the year. Books were few; religious periodicals
unknown. Doctrines, incidents, wonderful revival scenes of
manifested power were conveyed to each other in
conversations, in family circles, class meetings and love
feasts. What one knew all others soon learned. Presiding
elders usually recited in every love feast what had occurred
on the last round on their huge district, so that all knew the
state of the work, and were filled with joy and praise for what
God was doing everywhere.[12]

While serving in Philadelphia, Scott became acquainted
with the family of Ralph and Grace Smith, members of St.
George's. Their daughter, Sarah Ann, active in the congregation
since joining at age 17 in 1823, caught the young preacher's eye,
and his heart, and a courtship ensued. On November 22, 1830,
the couple was united in marriage by Levi's friend Anthony
Atwood. The couple would go on to have seven children, though
tragically, five would predecease them. In 1834, while living in
Chestertown, Maryland, Sarah fell dangerously ill, and never
fully recovered. For decades thereafter, she was largely confined
to her home, and often to her bed. Despite her condition, she
was remembered to have practiced a robust hospitality, opening
her home to visitors, especially to any itinerant preachers who
required housing, and was always eager to listen, "with intense
interest, to the recital of their toils, trials and triumphs."[13]

In 1830, Scott was ordained an elder, again in the
sanctuary of St. George's, by Bishop Elijah Hedding, and
assigned for the first time as preacher in charge, to West Chester
and Marshallton, in Chester County, Pennsylvania. One of the
duties of a circuit preacher was identifying and encouraging
young men who demonstrated potential to become itinerant
ministers. One such candidate was John A. Roche, a young
member and lay preacher of the Smyrna ME Church, during
Scott's tenure as preacher in charge of the circuit there in 1833.
Roche was resisting the invitation of Presiding Elder Solomon
Sharp to preach in revival services being held in Millington,
Maryland. Scott, newly appointed to the circuit, encouraged
Roche to go. Roche later wrote that he "yielded to the impor-
tunity of this holy man," and within a few years he joined the

An artist's rendering of St. George's ME Church, Philadelphia.
Built in 1767, it was acquired by the Methodists in 1769,
the first building owned by them in the city. St. George's
remained the center of regional Methodism for decades.
Here Scott was appointed to serve in 1828, ordained
a deacon the same year, and ordained an elder in 1830.
Here he also met his wife, Sarah, who was a member.

Left: Bishop Enoch George, who ordained Scott a deacon in 1828.
Right: Bishop Elijah Hedding, who ordained him an elder in 1830.

Philadelphia Conference. Roche later rose to prominence, filling major pulpits in Philadelphia and New York. Roche said of Scott, "His preaching was distinctive for clearness, soundness and unction, and there was a power that prostrated, roused and quickened the soul. He was an example of all he preached."[14]

Levi Scott as a Preacher

Accounts by colleagues suggest Scott's preaching style was neither florid nor highly rhetorical, but plain and logical, appealing to both head and heart. A statement read years later at Scott's funeral by preachers of the Philadelphia Conference, described his sermons as "clear, concise, direct, pointed, spiritual, experimental, practical, always moving, and sometimes overwhelming."[15] Roche characterized Scott as a theologically sound preacher, who "believed objective and subjective truth... With him inward grace was personal salvation, but it was through faith in essential doctrine." Roche recalled a sermon of Scott's at a camp meeting about 1835, while he was serving as presiding elder, on Revelation 20:11: "I saw a great white throne, and him that sat on it, from whose face the earth and the heaven fled away." Recalling that message fifty years later, Roche wrote:

Such was the sense of God's greatness awakened; such was the dazzling splendor of the "great white throne;" such was the impression of the vastness and composition of the assembly; such was the tremendous issues of the judgement; that even the most godly prayed that they might "find mercy in that day."[16]

A small book of Scott's sermon briefs survives in the collection at Barratt's Chapel, dating to 1835, when Scott was at "his zenith in pulpit power," according to Roche. One, entitled "Mary's Choice" (on Luke 10:42), reveals that Scott saw his own life as a circuit rider reflecting the pattern of Jesus himself:

Our blessed Lord was emphatically an itinerant preacher. He went about doing good, preaching the gospel of the kingdom, and healing all manner of sickness and all manner of disease among the people. Having no certain dwelling place, he ate and lodged with those friends who extended to him the hospitalities of their houses.

Though the book contains just a handful of sermons, they reveal Scott to be thoroughly Wesleyan in his message, emphasizing the need to respond in saving faith, along with the imperative of being sanctified by the power of the Holy Spirit. In one, entitled "Sanctification, the Will of God," Scott took aim at Calvinist pessimism about human potential in grace, and says,

Sanctification is your privilege. This is the will of God. He permits it – allows it – it is his good pleasure. He has no plan, no decree, no purpose, no disposition against it. There is nothing in his nature, or his government in opposition to it. The way then is fully open. There is no impediment. Nay, this is not all. God not only does not oppose, he desires it. It is his will. It is the end of all his dispensations toward us. For this end he spared not his own Son, but gave him up for us all. For this end he gave his word. For this end he sent his Spirit. For this end he instituted his ministry – his ordinances. All are intended to bring us to sanctification, and so to heaven... God invites and attracts us toward it by all the power of his love and dealings with us. Let us then yield to his sweet influences and sink into his arms.[17]

A Methodist camp meeting. These large, outdoor evangelistic gatherings were a staple of early 19th century Methodism. Preaching at them was a regular part of the duties of itinerants like Scott, both as a circuit preacher, and as a presiding elder.

Levi Scott stood five feet, eight inches tall, had grey-blue eyes, and reddish-brown hair which grew darker as he aged, and later was speckled with grey. As with St. Paul, he was said to be "unimpressive in appearance" (2 Cor. 10:10), and he loved to relate an incident that took place while on an episcopal tour in the Midwest in 1853. After arriving at the home of a Methodist family which had been expecting him, a young girl walked in the room where Scott was sitting, eyed him head to toe, then walked out. In the next room, within earshot of the bishop, she said to her mother, "Mother, is that the bishop? Why mother, he is nothing but a man, and not much of a man at that!"[18]

As that story suggests, Scott could be quite self-deprecating. Indeed, his writings and letters often indicate his own self-doubt as to his fitness for the offices he held. John Roche wrote of Scott that "a deep sense of his own incompetence often oppressed him, and he was sometimes on the eve of giving up the work." Apparently, Scott was determined to resign from his ministry during his second appointment, while serving on Dover Circuit. He met up with his presiding elder, Rev. Lawrence Lawrenson, who proceeded to share his own self-doubt and desire to step down from his post. Young Levi then pleaded with Lawrenson not to give up, that he was merely experiencing a temptation. In the process, Scott encouraged himself to stay with his ministry.[19]

His self-doubt continued into the episcopacy. In an 1856 letter to Rev. G. C. M. Roberts of Baltimore, Scott bemoaned "my short and I fear almost useless life."[20] To J. B. McCullough, Scott's genuine humility was "the most conspicuous of all his traits;" adding, "it may be said that he was humble to a fault."[21]

The Christian Advocate *of April 12, 1848 reported the sermon of Levi Scott during the Philadelphia Conference session, held the previous week:*

[A] large congregation assembled to hear... Rev. Levi Scott, DD, presiding elder of the South Philadelphia District. His discourse was founded upon the... words: "Study to show thyself approved unto God, a workman that needeth not to be ashamed, rightly dividing the word of truth" [2 Tim. 2:15]... [S]eldom has it been our good fortune to listen to a discourse so replete with sound, comprehensive, discriminating thought. We are very confident that the young men, to whom the chief portion of the sermon was directed, will do well to ponder upon and treasure up its teachings – the whole sum of which appeared to be to elevate the ministerial character by enforcing upon them the absolute necessity of showing themselves workmen approved unto God in all the duties and relations of their important office – in the study, the closet, the sick-room – when mingling with society, as well as when engaged in the official services of their calling; that the minister of Christ should be a type to others, and his example lead to heaven; that that he should not only, by diligent study and unwearied application, be thoroughly versed in the theory of his work, and by constant practice, added to the gifts of God, be skillful in its execution, but also become a personal laborer in giving it effect. No proxy can be allowed here. God calls no man to the ministry for the purpose of living in ease and idleness, but to constant, patient, and unceasing labor.

As a minister, Scott apparently tried to stifle his youthful love of "fun and frolic" (as he once put it), in order to assume the role of ordained pastor. His stern ideal for the demeanor and image of a man of God may be glimpsed in an 1876 tribute to his friend and colleague, Rev. Thomas J. Thompson, who embodied what Scott called "the twelve rules of a Methodist preacher." Bishop Scott then went on to enumerate those rules:

> Diligent, but never fussy; serious, never sour; avoiding lightness, jesting and foolish talking; prudent in his intercourse with all; free from suspicion and evil speaking; tender of the reputation of others; kind and faithful to those under his care; ashamed only of sin and meanness; punctual; a man of one work, and a true son in the gospel; asking nothing, declining nothing; and doing in good faith the work assigned to him.[22]

Scott never lost his sense of humor, however, as several contemporaries attest. In an 1827 letter to his brother John Lattomus, Scott ribbed him over complaints about not writing sooner, saying in part:

> The largest part... of your letter is taken up with a kind of semi-complaint because of my silence, to which I shall answer: Ha! I have drawn out Leviathan with a hook! A hook of silence! But my dear bro[ther], I did not voluntarily nor purposely throw out this hook, but necessity – necessity originating in the nature of my circumstances, caused me to drop it out at the side of the boat – and as it was dropped I am glad that it caught you, ha! Ha! If I could see you I would laugh right at you.[23]

Despite his grim ministerial ideal, and the grave bearing Scott strikes in extant photos, the old mischievous sense of humor broke through, especially in private. As John Roche put it, "in social life... [Scott] exhibited positive humor, and he possessed a keen sense of the ludicrous, and conscience did not always forbid its indulgence."[24]

John S. Inskip

Among Scott's more noteworthy converts was John S. Inskip, during Scott's tenure as pastor in charge of the West Chester and Marshallton Circuit, in Chester County, Pennsylvania. Inskip had been influenced by his father to scoff at Christianity, but as a teenager started having second thoughts, and began attending worship services as he sought answers. On April 10, 1832, at the Marshallton Church, Scott took as his text Luke 14:18, "And they all with one consent began to make excuse." While Scott was preaching, Inskip felt powerfully convicted. "The remark which rested with the greatest weight upon my mind," Inskip later said, "was... 'There is a little boy here who says that he is too young.' These words seem to say, 'Thou art the one to whom the word of this salvation is sent.'" Inskip determined to surrender his life to Christ, and at a second service in the church that evening, went forward during an altar call, found peace, and joined the church. Inskip would go on to become a prominent Methodist minister, a leader in the post-Civil War Holiness Movement, and president of the National Association for the Promotion of Holiness.[25]

Levi Scott, from a *carte de visite,* c. 1860.

3

Rising
Star

In April 1834, when just 31 years old, Levi Scott was
appointed presiding elder of the Delaware District. Southernmost of the Philadelphia Conference's seven districts, it
comprised about half of the Delmarva Peninsula, extending from
Cambridge, Maryland on the Chesapeake to Lewes, Delaware on
the coast, and down through the Virginia portion of the shore.
In his care were eight large circuits, taking in dozens of local
congregations, twenty-six Sunday schools, and nearly 13,000
members. During this era, when bishops were not yet stationed
geographically in specific conferences, presiding elders were
essentially sub-bishops, overseeing and administering the life of
the congregations in their care. The job involved constant travel
to preach, confer with preachers and congregations, fill
vacancies, recruit young men for the itineracy, and raise funds. A
primary duty was leading quarterly conference meetings – major
affairs during this era, in which all the outlying congregations of

a circuit came together to attend special preaching services, participate in love feasts, and conduct the business of the circuit. During Scott's two years on the district, the overall membership dipped slightly, but the district expanded to ten circuits and twenty-nine Sunday schools.[1]

In 1836, Scott was stationed in Newark, New Jersey, to lead the Franklin Street ME Church, a young congregation which had only recently completed its first house of worship, right across the street from city hall.[2] That same year, the churches in the state of New Jersey were separated from those in Pennsylvania and the Delmarva Peninsula to form the New Jersey Conference. In 1837, he returned to his old conference to take charge of Philadelphia's Ebenezer ME Church, which had lobbied the bishop for Scott to be appointed there. A later historian noted that Scott "emphasized in his preaching the doctrine of sanctification," and recorded that his first sermon was on the text, "For I am determined to know nothing among you save Jesus Christ and him crucified (1 Cor. 2:2)."[3] In 1839, Scott was transferred from Ebenezer, serving one year in charge of St. Paul's ME Church, also in the southern part of the city.

In 1840, Scott left pastoral ministry to serve as a teacher and administrator for Dickinson College, in Carlisle, Pennsylvania. Founded in 1783 by renowned Philadelphia physician Benjamin Rush, the college had struggled with financial strain and internal strife during the 1820s and early 1830s, until it temporarily closed its doors in 1832. The next year, the college was turned over to the Methodists of the Baltimore and Philadelphia Conferences, who rescued and revived it. In 1840, the college was under the presidency of Rev. John Price Durbin, and still struggling to become financially stable. Levi Scott became principal of Dickinson's grammar school, then a preparatory institution for those seeking admission to the college. He served there three years, shepherding forty to fifty students per year in their education, before returning to pastoral ministry. Even after resigning his post, he maintained ties with the school, serving as a trustee from 1858 until his death.[4]

Scott returned to Philadelphia in 1843 to serve as senior pastor of the Union ME Church on Fourth Street, then the preeminent pulpit in the region. With a membership of 1,000,

Philadelphia's Union ME Church, where Scott served, 1843-1845.

Union was one of the largest congregations in the conference, and frequently hosted the annual meeting of the Philadelphia Conference, including the session of 1844, midway through Scott's tenure at the church. Though Scott remained quiet during conference debates, infrequently taking the floor even to make motions, his colleagues clearly regarded him as a leader. They had already elected him as a delegate to the General Conference (the governing body of the denomination) in 1840, and would do so every four years until his elevation to the episcopacy.

After two years at Union, Scott was again appointed presiding elder, this time to the South Philadelphia District, which included the southern part of the city, and extended west to Harrisburg. While serving in this role, Scott took a special interest in the only black congregation on his district, Philadelphia's John Wesley ME Church. The congregation had undergone a split several years before, with many members joining the AME Church.[5] Those who remained were left with an unfinished building on Shippen Street, encumbered with nearly $2,000 in debt. Scott issued an appeal across the conference, which eventually made its way to the denominational paper, the New York-based *Christian Advocate*. "In recommending them to the benevolent public for assistance," Scott wrote, "I do think that if any people here or elsewhere deserve assistance, the people of 'John Wesley' Chapel do... If you cannot give them much, give a little. Drops, it is said, form the ocean; grains of sand the earth." The congregation survived, and is the direct ancestor of today's Tindley Temple United Methodist Church.[6]

Scott apparently spent quite a bit of time working with churches in deep financial holes. He gave considerable attention to the congregation in the city of Lancaster, Pennsylvania, which was so deep in debt, it was in danger of being sold at sheriff's sale. Scott met frequently with the trustees and other leaders, to give "advice and counsel in regard to the temporal interests of the society." He also appointed Rev. Andrew Manship to the charge in 1846. Known for his fundraising abilities, Manship later recalled going on "begging tours" to camp meetings around the conference to help save the property. The church endured, and is today's First United Methodist Church of Lancaster.[7]

Denominational Official

During the 1848 General Conference, Scott was elected Assistant Book Agent for the Methodist Episcopal Church, an administrative post with offices in New York City, where he moved his family that summer. Scott was second in command of the publishing arm of the denomination, working under the leadership of George Lane; all official publications of the church from 1848 to 1852 bear the imprint of "Lane and Scott."

Levi Scott and Women Leaders

While serving as pastor of the Union ME Church in Philadelphia, Levi Scott appointed Sarah Todd Elsegood to the post of class leader. She is believed to have been the first woman to hold that office in the Methodist Episcopal Church since its founding in 1784. Though they were fading from their earlier prominence in the life of American Methodism, class meetings were still a force within the Methodist Episcopal Church of the 1840s.

Sarah Todd Elsegood

Classes met weekly for spiritual instruction, accountability and prayer. The class leader held a position of spiritual authority over the souls in his – or in this case, her – care. Scott's own faith had been shaped by strong Christian women, notably Anne Scott and Betsy Carter. Scott's respect for the spiritual leadership capacity of women, born of personal experience, undoubtedly influenced his willingness to entrust Elsegood with such an important role. An account survives of Sarah's participation in revival services during the pastorate of Scott's successor, Rev. John Price Durbin. After Durbin had finished preaching, and issued his invitation for penitents to come forward to receive Christ, no one responded until he called upon "Sister Elsegood" to pray:

> The congregation knelt down. The melodious voice of this "Mother in Israel" rose in pleading, and reached the Throne. Sobs answered, tears fell, and before she ceased a great break occurred. People under conviction could not resist, and nearly fifty "mourners" were quickly at the altar.[8]

The Methodist Book Concern in New York, where
Scott served as Assistant Book Agent, 1848-1852.

It was a difficult time to be in leadership at the
publishing house, due to the schism which had occurred in
American Methodism four years before. At the six-week long
General Conference of 1844, held in New York City, delegates
had deadlocked over what to do about a slaveholding bishop
named James O. Andrew. In the end, the conference adopted a
formal "Plan of Separation," to allow the southern conferences to
form their own separate denomination. Part of the plan called
for an equitable division of the assets of the publishing house.
However, bitterness and controversy in the wake of the schism
created a backlash, and the constitutionally required ratification
of the plan by the individual annual conferences failed to
materialize. Delegates to the 1848 General Conference
pronounced the 1844 plan "null and void," essentially declaring
that the southern conferences had seceded, and therefore not
entitled either to a share of the assets, or to receive annual
dividends from the profits.

In response, the southern church sued the publishing
house. The case dragged on throughout Scott's tenure, requiring
much time and energy, both from him and George Lane. As it

turned out, the US District Court in New York found in favor of the South, and directed the publishing house to divide the assets. While Lane and Scott considered an appeal to the Supreme Court, one of its justices (who was also a Methodist layman), John McLean, intervened and arranged for a negotiated settlement, which was finalized in 1853.[9]

Despite the ongoing conflict, the publishing house grew. Sales in 1850 topped $250,000, prompting Lane and Scott to set a goal of $1,000,000 by 1856 – a goal which was met by their successors, Thomas Carlton and Zebulon Phillips. Of Scott's four-year tenure as Assistant Book Agent, a colleague who worked under him, Daniel P. Kidder, later wrote that Scott was not thrilled with the post, the duties of which, had been "submitted to by him, rather than enjoyed." Nonetheless, Kidder praised Scott as having "faithfully and discreetly performed" his work, "with a breadth of view that took in the full responsibility of providing a wholesome religious literature for a growing Church and her children."[10]

Bishop of the Church

By the spring of 1852, the Methodist Episcopal Church, now numbering nearly 750,000 members across the north, was down from five to just three effective bishops: Thomas A. Morris, Edmund S. Janes and Beverly Waugh. Bishop Elijah Hedding, on his deathbed, would pass away just three weeks before the General Conference that year, and Bishop Leonidas Hamline had announced his intention to resign for health reasons. The rapidly growing denomination needed new episcopal leadership, and Levi Scott had grown in stature and reputation across the church during his four years as Assistant Book Agent. As early as his appointment to that post in 1848, Scott's name had been lifted up as "bishop timber." His wife, Sarah, wrote him that year, "Did I not tell you, you were going to be made bishop?"[11]

So it came to be. To the 1852 General Conference, held in Boston, Scott came as the favored son of the Philadelphia Conference, and strongly supported by New York, where he had lived for four years, preaching frequently in the churches of the

Bishops of the ME Church, 1848. Back row, Edmund Janes, Leonidas Hamline; front, Thomas Morris, Elijah Hedding, Beverly Waugh. By the General Conference of 1852, Hedding was dead and Hamline had resigned, requiring new bishops to be elected.

----

city. On the first ballot, held on Tuesday, May 25, four new bishops were elected, and Scott was at the head of the list with 113 votes, followed by Matthew Simpson (110), Osmond C. Baker of New England (90) and Edward R. Ames of Ohio (89).[12]

Nineteenth-century bishops were not, as today, assigned to particular geographical areas; the episcopacy within American Methodism did not assume its present diocesan form until 1912. Like the preachers they supervised, bishops were also itinerants, spending their time traveling around the country. They superintended annual conference sessions, dedicated churches, spoke at camp meetings and other special events, and became familiar with the leading citizens of all the major cities across the nation – which, incidentally, gave the bishops social and political influence, as would become clear later during the Civil War. After his consecration as bishop, Scott chose Wilmington, Delaware for his family's residence, no doubt in part from loyalty to his home state, but also because of its convenience as a transportation hub. He would spend long periods away from home in the exercise of his duties.

The work could be grueling. In 1853, for example, Bishop Scott spent the first part of the year in Liberia, on the west coast of Africa, arriving home May 10 after a five-week trans-Atlantic voyage. He picked up his work among the conferences by convening the Wisconsin Conference in late August, followed by the Rock River (Chicago) Conference beginning September 14; then came in succession the Iowa Conference (September 28), Illinois (October 12) and South Illinois (October 26), before returning home.[13]

The traveling was difficult. Roads frequently were poor, and travel by rail or sail was hazardous. In the summer of 1858, while on an episcopal tour of the west coast, Scott was aboard the steamer *Sierra Nevada*, bound from San Francisco to Port Townsend, Washington Territory, when a storm damaged the ship. A passenger drowned, as did several livestock, prompting the bishop to write his wife, "For four days it was doubtful whether any of us would ever again see the land." On the next leg of his journey, he was aboard the steamer *Constitution*, when it ran aground in the Bay of Victoria.[14] In 1870, while traveling by rail to New Orleans, his train derailed crossing a drawbridge over a bayou, but somehow did not fall into the water. "The jar was terrible," he wrote home, "but we were safe. If the engine had gone off we should probably all have been drowned."[15]

Compounding the risks of travel was Scott's delicate health. From an early age, he showed a susceptibility to sickness. Twice in his early ministerial career he was forced temporarily to cease traveling for health reasons. After his third year in ministry, while serving in Philadelphia, his health broke down; the charge at St. George's, however, was so fond of him that they asked for his return a second year, then granted Scott a five-month vacation to recover. In 1832, his health again failing, he asked for "supernumerary" status within the conference – akin to a medical leave of absence – and was off for eight months. In

Bishops Matthew Simpson (left) and Osmond C. Baker, who
were elected along with Scott at the 1852 General Conference.

----

early 1833, he resumed preaching, this time near his family
home, on the Smyrna Circuit. Later that spring he returned to
the itinerant ranks, and was assigned to the Kent, Maryland
Circuit. His health still delicate, Scott's appointment there was
considered "light work" – it was only an eleven-point charge![6]

While in Liberia in 1853, Scott contracted an illness,
nowhere named, but probably malaria, for he suffered its effects
throughout his life thereafter. Scott's extant letters often speak
of his being "prostrated" with illness for weeks or months at a
time. Friends and colleagues marveled not only that he lived as
long as he did, but that he was able to serve so long as an
effective itinerant bishop. A colleague who knew him fifty years
remarked that, in answer to questions about health, he never
once recalled hearing "I am well" come from Scott's lips. "He was
never well," the colleague continued; "[and] it was a perpetual
doubt... whether his health was sufficient for the work. This was
the weighty question when he was named for bishop."[7]

A Letter Home

Steamer Panama, Esquimalt Harbor, Vancouver Island,
July 24th, 1858

My dear Wife:

I left San Francisco the 10th inst., in the steamer *Sierra Nevada* for Port Townsend, and after a most stormy passage of 7 days, arrived at the port of destination on the 17th. For four days, it was doubtful whether any of us would ever again see the land. We lost a mule and four horses and two beeves, washed overboard or drowned – and worse than all, one poor fellow, a carpenter from San Francisco, fell overboard and was drowned. The ship was a good deal broken, and greatly strained, particularly in her upper works. But God brought us safely to port. I spent the Sabbath at Port Townsend, and preached in the afternoon. Monday at 8 AM, I took the steamer *Constitution* for Olympia at the head of the sound via Bellingham, Bay of Victoria. Both those places we visited, but going out of the harbor of Victoria on Tuesday night the 20th inst., the steamer was run upon the rocks and stuck fast. I left her in a small boat with several men and returned to Victoria from which the accident occurred about one mile distant...

I have reached the farthest limit of my course, and have now turned my face homeward, so that every move I now make will bring me towards home, from which, should the Lord spare me to reach it, I think I shall never go again on "the wide, wide sea." I hope you all remember me in your prayers. My chief consolation when we were likely to go to a watery grave was that I should sink at my post.

My love and warmth to the children,

Yours as ever,
L. Scott

An engraving of Bishop Scott which appeared in
the January 1856 issue of the *Ladies' Repository*.

4

Levi Scott and Slavery

In addition to his health, another weighty question facing Scott upon his consecration as bishop was that of slavery, over which the nation – and the Methodist Episcopal Church – grew increasingly polarized in the 1850s. Of the four bishops elected in 1852, Levi Scott was the only one who had been reared in a slave state.[1] The unique way slavery evolved in Delaware, coupled with Scott's personal and family experiences, produced in him a genuine empathy toward free and enslaved blacks, while at the same time prevented him from embracing a full-fledged abolitionism.

In the 1600s, the early colonial settlements in Delaware were among the first of the future states of the Union to become heavily dependent on African slave labor. Indeed, in British-dominated North America, Delaware and New York became "the first significant homes of American slavery north of Spanish Florida."[2] By the eve of the American Revolution, an estimated one-fifth to one-fourth of Delaware's population were African slaves or their descendants. With the American Revolution came the assertion of those self-evident truths of liberty, equality and the natural rights of all men. The contradiction between slavery and the rhetoric of liberty was not lost on the founding generation. Northern states not as heavily dependent on slave labor for their economies began passing laws allowing for a process of gradual emancipation, beginning with Pennsylvania in 1780. Delaware, however, would retain legally protected slavery, along with the states of the deep South, until the Civil War forced an end to the institution.[3]

Nevertheless, in Delaware slavery developed in a very different manner than it did elsewhere, and was already withering in Levi Scott's youth. The state's climate was not well suited to growing cotton, nor did its land produce the best quality tobacco, the two most labor-intensive crops, for which slavery was most profitably employed. Delaware's primary cash crops were corn and wheat, grown largely for sale in the Philadelphia market. Farmers often found that it was cheaper to hire temporary workers than to house, feed and clothe slaves year-round. In addition, the typical Delaware slave owner possessed a relative handful of slaves on a small family farm, and by necessity, slave and master often worked the fields together. In the Delaware that Levi Scott knew growing up, blacks and whites, slave and free, worked, lived, and worshipped in close proximity, developing complex, even intimate, relationships across lines of race, as Scott's conversion story demonstrates. Another blow to slavery came in the form of laws passed in Delaware, beginning in 1787, that effectively banned the sale of slaves beyond the state border. Over time this greatly reduced the economic value of the state's enslaved population, undermining the long-term viability of slavery.[4]

There was also the influence of Methodism on the peninsula, which in its early days was second only to the Quakers in its outspoken opposition to slavery. Early Methodists took their cue from John Wesley, who in 1774 published *Thoughts Upon Slavery*, an adaptation of an anti-slavery tract written by Philadelphia Quaker Anthony Benezet. At its founding in December 1784, the Methodist Episcopal Church in America passed a rule requiring all its members to provide for

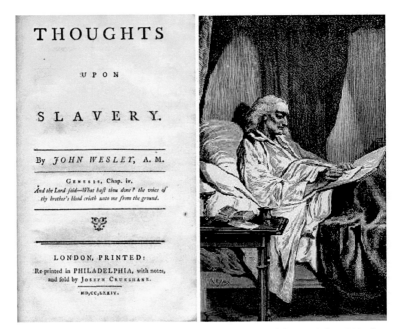

THOUGHTS

UPON

SLAVERY.

By *JOHN WESLEY*, A. M.

GENESIS, Chap. iv.

And the Lord said—What haft thou done? the voice of thy brother's blood crieth unto me from the ground.

LONDON, PRINTED:

Re-printed in PHILADELPHIA, with notes, and sold by JOSEPH CRUKSHANK.

MD,CC,LXXIV.

Left: John Wesley's 1774 anti-slavery pamphlet. Right: Wesley writing his last known letter (1791) to anti-slavery parliament-arian William Wilberforce, urging him to *"Go on, in the name of God, and in the power of his might, till even American slavery (the vilest that ever saw the sun) shall vanish away before it."*

----

the freedom of their slaves within a year or face expulsion. Though this rule was later suspended, and the church increasingly accommodated itself to slavery, for decades Methodist ministers preached against the institution, encouraged lay members to free their slaves, and even lobbied state legislatures to pass emancipation laws.[5]

In Delaware, the impact of early anti-slavery Methodism was profound, especially since the movement made significant inroads among the upper classes. Lay Methodists among the gentry, like Andrew Barratt and Richard Bassett, emancipated their slaves, and became active in efforts to abolish slavery. It was Richard Bassett, later a governor of Delaware and US Senator, who introduced to the General Assembly the 1787 law prohibiting the sale of slaves beyond state borders. He was also a founder of the Delaware Society for Promoting the Abolition of

Slavery (1788). Historian William H. Williams observed, "most Delaware Methodists freed their slaves during the years 1775 to 1810." By 1810, when Levi Scott was eight years old, seventy six percent of the black population of Delaware was free.[6]

In addition, there was Scott's family heritage. His maternal grandparents, named March, were English-born, and settled on a farm in Kent County, Maryland, about eight miles from Chestertown. There Levi's mother grew up with her seven siblings in a slaveholding family. The 1785 will of Anne's father, John March, bequeathed to his daughter Mary "a Negro boy called Will," and to his daughter Araminta, "a Negro boy named Solomon."[7] Levi's father, however, was the son of Scots-Irish immigrants, large numbers of whom were brought to Delaware as indentured servants in the eighteenth century, sometimes against their will. In fact, there may have been as many unfree white laborers in the state as black ones during that era, and the treatment of the former group was little better than that of the latter. Delaware newspapers list many more white runaways than black ones prior to the Revolution. These Scots-Irish servants, along with some southern Irish, Scots, and Germans, were regarded by the English and the Anglicized Dutch and Swedish gentry as "a troublesome and inferior people who needed to be kept in their place."[8]

Levi's grandparents, John and Lydia Scott, arrived in America before the Revolution, though it is not known if John was an indentured servant. Even so, he would have felt the prevailing prejudice against the ethnically, culturally, and religiously alien Scots-Irish. Levi was only a generation removed from living memories of social disapproval and discrimination in his family, which likely created in him a natural affinity toward the plight of African Americans. Another indication of anti-slavery sentiment in his family is suggested by the actions of his step-uncle, Rev. James Lattomus, brother of Anne's Scott's first husband, and a clergy member of the Philadelphia Conference. Lattomus presented a petition to the 1800 General Conference of the ME Church, which would have required all lay members of the church to emancipate their slaves within a year.[9]

Even more, African Americans had been the agents of Scott's early faith formation. Already noted was his conversion

Left: Jarena Lee, a female evangelist who preached in Scott's hometown in 1823. Right: Rev. Adam Wallace.

----

in the home of free blacks Isaac and Betsy Carter. In addition, Scott likely was present the summer after his conversion experience when evangelist Jarena Lee preached in the school house in Cantwell Bridge. The first black female preacher in the United States, Lee frequently crossed racial and denominational lines and was acclaimed by whites and blacks alike. In her 1849 autobiography, she describes preaching there in July 1823, "[I] spoke in a School house, from Math, xxii, 41 – 'What think ye of Christ?' The presence of the Lord overshadowed us – believers rejoiced – some were awakened to believe well of my Master, and I trust are on their way to glory."[10] Scott's experiences at this formative stage of his faith instilled in him a respect for the spiritual and leadership capacities of blacks, which would be borne out in his work as a bishop in the 1850s and 1860s.

An incident from 1854 sheds light on his sympathies. A young preacher named Adam Wallace was in charge of the Northampton Circuit on the Eastern Shore of Virginia, during a time of increasing polarization over slavery and race. Wallace antagonized white members by reviving the customary quarterly reading of the General Rules of the ME Church, which included a prohibition against "the buying or selling the bodies and souls of men, women or children, with an intention to enslave them." Worse, Wallace insisted that black members of the churches come down from the galleries to the same altar as whites during communion services, and declared, "at this one point, all social distinction must vanish." Congregants stormed out, and leading members pressured Wallace to change his ways, with the implied threat that he might need to leave town. Just then, Bishop Scott happened to visit the area during a tour of the peninsula, and the question was put to him whether Wallace should send the elements to the galleries, as leading members demanded. As Wallace recalled it, Bishop Scott, "in his usually deliberative way, [said] 'I would not do it.'" Such was the respect with which Scott was held by Methodists of the lower Peninsula that his decision stood, and Wallace remained at his post.[11]

Gradual Emancipationist

Yet Scott was not an abolitionist, at least not a "modern abolitionist," as detractors often described those aligned with the movement which William Lloyd Garrison and others brought to prominence in the 1830s. Rather, Scott's attitude reflected the culture of the Philadelphia Conference in this era. In the 1830s and 1840s, as Garrisonian abolitionism pressed for immediate and uncompensated emancipation, the Philadelphia Conference found itself in a delicate position. Until the end of the Civil War, it contained within its bounds both slave and free territory. Pennsylvania, of course, was a free state; Philadelphia, home to the nation's largest population of free blacks, was a center of refuge and relief for fugitives seeking liberty. But the conference also included the state of Delaware and the Eastern Shore territories of the slave states of Maryland and Virginia.

Scott was a delegate to the General Conference of 1844, which resulted in the ME Church splitting into northern and southern denominations. This rupture came after decades of growing polarization within the national body over slavery. By 1840, three perspectives or groups had crystalized within the

Bishop Edmund S. Janes,
(1807-1876), who was
elected bishop in 1844
from the Philadelphia
Conference because
he was a moderate on
slavery, and thus able
to garner southern votes.

Methodist Episcopal Church. One consisted of the abolitionists, led by men like Rev. Orange Scott of New England, whose message was simple: slavery was sin and needed to be eliminated from both church and society. Abolitionists were a small minority within the church, enjoying numerical strength only in New England. A second group was comprised of people who believed slavery consistent with Christian faith. It was either morally neutral, and only problematic when slaves were mistreated; or even a positive good, ordained by God to Christianize and civilize Africans. This mindset predominated among the membership of the annual conferences within the southern slaveholding states. A third group of ministers and laity, which constituted the majority of northern Methodists, attempted to steer a middle course, considering themselves anti-slavery, but not abolitionist.

This last view dominated the culture of the Philadelphia Conference, which by 1842 had developed a policy of excluding from its ministerial ranks both slave owners and outspoken abolitionists. In so doing, they sought to avoid both extremes in the debate: the "proslaveryists" on the on hand, and "ultra-abolitionists" on the other, as conference members often referenced the antagonists. It is worth noting that Philadelphia Conference member Edmund S. Janes was one of the last two men elected bishop by a united church during the 1844 General

Conference, before splitting north and south. As a "moderate" on slavery, Janes was acceptable enough to southern delegates to garner the votes needed to win election to the episcopacy.[12]

In the aftermath of the schism, the Philadelphia Conference became a "border conference," in which spiritual jurisdiction of its southernmost territories was bitterly contested by both branches of Methodism. Local churches divided, preachers were sometimes driven out of town, and even mob violence marked church life on the Delmarva portion of the conference in the 1840s.[13] To retain the loyalty of its churches on the peninsula, the Philadelphia Conference tried to maintain its moderating position, rejecting both the pro-slavery theology that was becoming more strident and sophisticated in the South, and the abolitionist movement, which was generating enormous controversy in the north.[14]

This attitude within the conference was exemplified by a man whom evidence suggests was something of a mentor to Levi Scott, despite how close in age the two men were. Well-educated and eloquent, Rev. John Price Durbin was the most distinguished and respected member of the Philadelphia Conference in the 1840s. His career included stints as president of Dickinson College, editor of the *Christian Advocate*, Chaplain of the US Senate, and, later, many years as chief executive of the denomination's Missionary Society. It was Durbin, as president of Dickinson, who had convinced Scott to leave the itineracy and join the faculty and administration of the college. Durbin and Scott served together on successive General Conference delegations, and the two men had voted together at the 1844 General Conference to support a proposal which would have would have required Bishop James O. Andrew either to rid himself of his slaves, or to leave the episcopacy.[15]

To Durbin, slavery was an evil blight upon the land which ought to be abolished; Methodism was in fact, anti-slavery, yet it could not embrace "modern abolitionism," which was too radical in its demand for immediate, uncompensated emancipation. This could only result in further schism and violence. Durbin argued that there was no New Testament warrant to exclude slaveholders from membership in the church, and that toleration of slavery had been necessary to allow the

Rev. John Price Durbin, leading member of the Philadelphia Conference and colleague of Levi Scott. They shared similar views on slavery and its abolition (*Dickinson College*).

----

church to become established in the South. Along with many clergy of his day, Durbin believed that, as slaves and owners alike were brought into the fold of the church, the influence of the gospel, along with the national ideals of liberty and equality, would eventually dismantle the institution.[16] That Scott shared this perspective is confirmed by his son-in-law, who wrote:

> The nation had seen the workings of gradual emancipation in the case of the northern slave states, and supposed that like policy would succeed in relieving the territory yet encumbered with slavery... The large majority of the nation were in that day gradual emancipationists... This was the position and view of Mr. Scott, and with him stood multitudes of the best men of the nation.[17]

The problem was that, by the 1840s, the economic and cultural tides had shifted, and slavery was growing more entrenched, not less. There had been a sea change in public opinion, and in church culture, between 1810 and 1850. Racial theories positing African inferiority were given pseudo-scientific bases that did not exist before. Anti-slavery societies in the South evaporated, and northern states passed laws restricting or revoking black voting rights – including Pennsylvania, which disfranchised its free black population in 1838. Pro-slavery theology acquired influential, intellectual spokesmen such as Rev. William Capers of South Carolina (later a bishop), and Dr. William A. Smith, president of Randolph-Macon College. Eastern Shore blacks and whites gradually ceased worshipping together as members of the same congregation, with African Americans increasingly founding their own churches.

As an example of the cultural shift, in 1826 the leadership of the circuit centered in Cambridge, Maryland sent a resolution to the Philadelphia Conference during its annual session that year. The document called for an end to slavery, declaring it a "national evil... [and] a most evident violation of the fundamental principles of Christianity." In 1861, the same quarterly conference publicly called for separation from the Pennsylvania portion of the conference to protect the "peculiar institution."[8] Men like Scott and Durbin, who had been reared in border states (Durbin was a Kentuckian), and in their formative years had witnessed progress toward the elimination of slavery, did not seem to fully grasp how attitudes were hardening. They found themselves seeking to occupy a moderate, middle ground during an era of polarization in which the middle was fast dropping out.

The Colonization Movement

One way Scott funneled his anti-slavery impulses was to support the colonization movement, which advocated that free blacks in America emigrate to Africa and create there a democratic republic which would demonstrate their competence for freedom, and fitness for full citizenship in America. Largely through the efforts of the American Colonization Society (ACS), established in 1816, the colony of Liberia was founded on the

An engraving of a meeting of the American Colonization Society
in Washington DC, with orator Edward Everett speaking.

west coast of Africa in the 1820s, and soon established its capital
at Monrovia (named for US President James Monroe). Between
1820 and 1860, some 10,000 African Americans relocated to
Liberia, which adopted an American-style constitution in 1847,
and elected its first president that same year.

The colonization movement has been criticized sharply,
both during the nineteenth century and by modern historians,
as simply providing cover for slaveholders whose real agenda
was to rid themselves of troublesome free blacks. Other critics
have simply dismissed the movement as salve for the guilty
consciences of whites who sympathized with the enslaved, but
could not bring themselves to embrace abolitionism.[19] During
the antebellum period, however, the picture was more
complicated. Although denounced by leading abolitionists like
William Lloyd Garrison, the movement was supported by others,
including Thomas Garrett of Delaware, whose home was part of
the Underground Railroad, and who was credited with helping
thousands of fugitives make their way to freedom.[20] Most
African Americans rejected colonization; not long after the ACS

was founded, prominent African Methodist leader Richard Allen led a meeting in Philadelphia of 2,000 free blacks who publicly condemned the ACS, convinced that its agenda actually would prolong slavery. Some African Americans, however, did support colonization, notably Daniel Coker, who with Allen had been among the principal founders of the AME Church. Coker sailed to Liberia himself in 1820, among the first shipload of colonists.[21]

For many anti-slavery whites, colonization offered a way to demonstrate the capacity of African Americans for self-government and the obligations of full citizenship, free from the fetters of slavery and discrimination so endemic in America. For others opposed to slavery, the racism of society was so deep and intractable that the only hope for a life of dignity and opportunity was to leave the United States. This last line of thinking resonated within the black community for an additional reason: the tenuous nature of the liberty which even free blacks enjoyed in the antebellum United States. There was always the danger that free African Americans could be kidnapped, declared to be fugitives and sold into bondage. In Delaware, the infamous Patty Cannon gang abducted scores of free blacks in the region during the early decades of the nineteenth century, before her death in a Sussex county jail in 1829. Prominent African Methodist leader Richard Allen was once abducted on a Philadelphia street and nearly re-enslaved, only avoiding that fate because of his prominence in the city.[22]

Bishop Scott supported the colonization movement. For decades he held membership in the American Colonization Society, and supported it financially. Several annual conferences within the Methodist Episcopal Church endorsed and financially supported the colonization movement. Among them was the Philadelphia Conference, which in 1834 appointed the fourth of July as the annual date for a conference-wide offering to support the ACS and affiliated bodies.[23] The colonization movement continued to garner widespread support into the Civil War, and even beyond. Abraham Lincoln was an advocate, and appointed none other than Levi Scott's son-in-law (and later biographer), James Mitchell, as head of the Federal Emigration Office, charged with overseeing the administration's colonization policy. Mitchell had emigrated from Northern Ireland in the

Left: An image believed to be that of Daniel Coker, one of the
founders of the AME Church, and early émigré to Liberia.
Right: Rev. James Mitchell, Levi Scott's son-in-law, who served
in the Lincoln administration as director of the Federal
Immigration Office *(National Archives)*.

1830s, and married the bishop's daughter Emma. Before the war,
Mitchell had served as Colonization Agent for the state of
Indiana, and first met Lincoln in 1853. As Lincoln's point-man on
colonization policy, Mitchell spent two frustrating years in
unsuccessful efforts to resettle free blacks to colonies in the
Caribbean and Latin America.[24] Looking back years later at his
and Bishop Scott's support of colonization, Mitchell described
the movement as an attempt to "heal with half-measures," yet
insisted that it had been undertaken "in an unselfish spirit to
avoid the evils of civil war, relieve the oppressed slave, and give
Christian civilization to Africa."[25]

The Mount Scott United Methodist Church, in Liberia,
named in honor of Bishop Levi Scott, whose 1853 visit
there was the first by a bishop of the ME Church.

5

Journey to Liberia

However we evaluate Scott's support of colonization, there can be no question of his concern for the men and women of color who emigrated to Africa. Among the first challenges he took on as a newly elected bishop was a transatlantic trip to Liberia, in order to superintend the church's mission conference there. Many of the colonists who settled in Liberia were Methodists, and had been members of the ME or AME churches; Daniel Coker had actually organized the first Methodist society for Liberia while at sea. Lay leaders and local preachers among the settlers soon began asking for help from America, to support and staff congregations, and assist outreach efforts to the native population. In late 1832, the Missionary Society of the ME Church sent Rev. Melville B. Cox as its first missionary to Liberia. Of frail health, Cox died just months after his arrival, but managed in that short time to establish the first Sunday school, the first camp meeting, and a rudimentary conference structure, employing lay preachers already there. In 1836, the General Conference officially recognized the work in Liberia as a Mission Conference of the Methodist Episcopal Church, the first to be so designated.[1]

The mission in Liberia advanced in fits and starts through the years, hampered by lack of resources, frequent leadership changes (often due to the ravages of disease), and complicated relations with native tribes. By the early 1850s, the conference was without adequate leadership and direction from the mother church, and was pressing for help. The 1852 General Conference gave considerable attention to the situation in Liberia. At its close, the board of bishops determined to send one of their number to Africa to personally inspect the work, offer guidance, and report back with recommendations. Newly elected Bishop Levi Scott offered himself to make the journey, and plans were made for him to leave in late fall, to be present during the dryer, cooler, winter months.

Travel by sea was perilous, and the Liberian mission had already proven notoriously deadly to American missionaries, so Scott prepared to leave fully aware he might never return. After a tearful farewell to his family on November 26, Scott was escorted to the Wilmington train station by his friends and colleagues, Revs. John Roche, Andrew Manship, and Joshua Humphries. He arrived that evening amid a drenching rain at the Baltimore home of Bishop Beverly Waugh, where Scott lodged until embarking the next day. Waugh left an account of Scott's departure, noting in part:

> In view of the peril of the ocean, and the still greater perils on the land, he gave evidence that he had adopted the sentiments of the Apostles, and could give them utterance in the words, "But none of these things move me, neither count I my life dear unto myself, so that I might finish my course with joy, and the ministry which I have received of the Lord Jesus, to testify to the gospel of the grace of God." Noble sentiment! Noble man! May his divine Master preserve, guide and bless him in all his ways and in all his works, and bring him again to the safety of health to his family and friends.[2]

Left: Rev. Andrew Manship, a close friend and colleague who
saw Scott off from Wilmington, as he left for Africa.
Right: Bishop Beverly Waugh, with whom Scott lodged in
Baltimore the night before his ship set sail for Liberia.

Scott spent six weeks aboard the bark *Shirley* making the
crossing, arriving at the harbor near Monrovia on January 6. He
kept a journal of the voyage, in which he describes in great detail
the weather, sightings of various sea creatures, the work of the
crew, and several major storms which threatened the vessel. He
also notes preaching services held on Sundays, a service in which
he baptized six children of passengers, and a funeral at sea he
led for a crewman. There are also frequent entries in which he
muses about his distant family. His entry for December 25 reads:

> Christmas with summer heat! Wonder what sort of day at
> home... Our children are now, I suppose (six AM Wilmington
> time), just beginning to look up their Christmas presents.
> The Lord bless them and their mother and all, and give them
> a happy Christmas. I, too, got a Christmas present this
> morning. I found under my plate a note, containing a very
> neat marker, with the words handsomely worked in,
> "Jehovah-Jirah." It was from Miss Freeman.[3]

Service at Sea

Bishop Scott's journal of his Liberia journey is filled with observations on the sights and sounds of the sea. An entry for Sunday, December 12, 1852 describes a shipboard worship experience. (Above: image of a 19th century bark or barque, defined by the number of masts and style of rigging.)

Twelve PM. Have just closed a very pleasant religious service. Brother Scott read the hymns and Scripture, and Brother Horne delivered a very appropriate discourse on John 13:6. The singing was led by two Grebo youths, who have been educated in the States by the Missionary Society of the Protestant Episcopal Church, and are now returning to their native land as missionaries. They sing delightfully. I felt it very pleasant to worship God amid his wonders on the deep. Never before did I listen to a sermon under like circumstances. The officers and crew, passengers, and emigrants were assembled on the quarter-deck. I sat on the starboard side, my chair placed against a water hogshead, and facing the northeast. The large swells, at least two hundred yards from summit to summit, rose up before me, closing the whole field of vision in that direction, and then the bark gently mounting aloft, I could look down into the vast vale below, the bark at the same time running at the rate of from seven to nine knots.

The *Shirley* reached the Liberian coast on January 6. "What a scene spread out before me!" Scott later recalled.

> There was Cape Mesurado, though in midwinter, clad with a rich and gorgeous vegetation. From the summit of the lighthouse floated the star and stripes of the African republic, while beyond, on the highest ground, in full view, was our seminary, perhaps the most substantial structure of Monrovia and all the African colonies.[4]

Coming ashore, Scott was greeted by Rev. Francis Burns, an émigré who had served for years as a presiding elder, and had been in de facto charge of the conference. On Sunday, Scott preached his first sermon in Liberia, on Acts 2:39: "For the promise is to you and your children, and them that are far off, even as many as the Lord our God will call." In the audience was the president of Liberia, Joseph J. Roberts, with his wife, "each having a Bible and hymn book." Also present was the vice president, Anthony Williams, who had been a Methodist preacher in Virginia before emigrating in 1823.[5]

Scott remained in the country two months, visiting its settlements, preaching in its churches, meeting with native leaders, examining financial and property matters, and inaugurating changes in the organization of the conference. Among his innovations was a redesign of the educational system among the children of both the settlers and the natives, which had been failing. Instead of American-style schools, which had difficulty retaining both students and teachers, Scott proposed a mentoring system in which not more than five children would lodge with a married preacher and his family for not less than four years, with funding and accountability to come through the office of the presiding elder. This new system was followed successfully, and known for years as the "Scott Schools."[6]

On Monday, March 7, 1853 in Monrovia, Bishop Scott convened the annual session of the Liberia Annual Conference, with fifteen preachers in attendance the first day. The conference lasted eight days, and was the first presided over by a bishop of the ME Church outside the continental United States. On the second day of the conference, Scott received into full

A mid-19th century view of Monrovia from the harbor, as it would have greeted Bishop Scott on his arrival. Scott's visit in the winter of 1853 helped reinvigorate the Methodist mission in Liberia.

----

conference membership ordained elders of the AME Church, ruling that "the spirit of the *Discipline*, though not the letter," allowed for this precedent. On Sunday, March 13, "under the shade of tamarind and mango-plum trees... [before] a large and attentive congregation," he ordained thirteen deacons and eight elders – the first time that black preachers in the Methodist Episcopal Church were ordained and received into full membership during an annual conference session.[7]

Bishop Scott departed from Liberia March 18, again aboard the *Shirley*. As before, he detailed in his journal the sights and dangers of the voyage, including a sea-borne tornado that nearly swamped the ship shortly after its departure. He had a companion with him for the return voyage, a pet monkey he was given while on shore, whom he named "Afric." The monkey apparently helped relieve the monotony of the voyage for the good bishop, who writes of nursing the animal through a bout of sickness – which included "a half-gill of port wine" that left the monkey somewhat tipsy. Scott also was called upon to officiate at another funeral, this time for the captain of the ship, George Chase, on April 11. "There is something repulsive in the idea of being buried in the sea," Scott mused in his journal afterward; "But what matters it? '*The sea gave up the dead which were in it;*' ocean, as earth, may conceal our mortal remains from the view of our fellows, but not from the eye of Him who 'Watches all our dust/ Till he shall bid it rise.'"[8] The ship arrived in Baltimore harbor on the morning of May 10, and Scott then made his way home to Wilmington by noon, where he found his family well. "O that men would praise the Lord for his goodness," the bishop entered into his journal, quoting Psalm 107:8, "and for his wonderful works to the children of men!"[9]

According to historian Wade Crawford Barclay, Scott's visit to Liberia "served in large part to revitalize the work and hearten the workers."[10] To this day, the Mount Scott United Methodist Church, in Maryland County, Liberia, is named in honor of Bishop Scott. For his part, Scott seems to have been profoundly affected by the visit. In a speech given before the Missionary Society after his return, Scott said,

> I preached at all the different settlements, and I found there the same God and the same religion which I enjoyed in my native land. I spent many joyous and happy days among these sons of Ham. I confess frankly, that while there, I lost all prejudice on account of color, and had not the peculiarity of the climate been such as to require me to sleep on board the vessel, I would have lodged with them most cheerfully.[11]

Upon his return, Scott reported to his fellow bishops, and made recommendations for the future of the work in Liberia. Among them was a call for stronger on-site supervision of the conference from among the colonists themselves, rather than in the form of appointed white missionaries from overseas. While still on in Liberia, Scott had written in his journal:

> There is a great need of firm, vigorous and judicious [church] government here. We must have a superintendent, white or colored, and I incline strongly to the latter... Before a white superintendent can get his plans fully matured or carried into practical effect, his health declines, and he dies or leaves the country. Then, after a longer or shorter interval, another

Left: Joseph J. Roberts, first president of Liberia, 1848-1856. Scott reported that Roberts "received me very kindly." Right: Rev. Francis Burns, in whose company Scott spent much time in Liberia. Burns later became the first black bishop in the ME Church.

----

comes, and some new measures are adopted and carried into half effect; then another, etc... I find, too, that our people here desire a colored superintendent. They cannot see why this may not be when all their civil and military officers are colored men.[12]

Accordingly, delegates to the next General Conference, held in 1856, voted to create the office of Missionary Bishop, to allow the Liberian Conference to elect its own episcopal leader, whose authority to preside would be limited to the continent of Africa. Because this required a constitutional change, concurring votes of the annual conferences were required. Once these were obtained, the Liberian Conference elected Francis Burns, who had been singled out for his faithfulness and competence by Bishop Scott. Burns came to the United States for consecration at the hands of his fellow bishops in 1858. Francis Burns was the first black bishop in the Methodist Episcopal Church.[13]

Conferences of Colored Preachers

The General Conference of 1856 took yet another action that would affect the status of black preachers in the Methodist Episcopal Church, and in which Scott would play an important role. During the 1848 General Conference, a petition had been presented by Scott's colleague and mentor, John P. Durbin, to authorize bishops to convene and preside over annual conferences of black preachers. Delegates demurred that year, but authorized bishops to "employ colored preachers... where their services are considered necessary." Four years later, a similar petition was received, and the General Conference again declined to create annual conferences in which black preachers could enjoy full clergy rights. However, it did authorize bishops to convene an annual assembly of black lay preachers for the purpose of "promoting... [and] assigning them their work." No bishop did so, though a "Convention of Colored Preachers" was held in Philadelphia's Zoar ME Church that year, without episcopal supervision.[14]

African Americans, both slave and free, had been an integral part of American Methodism from its inception as an organized movement in the 1760s. Large numbers of blacks were attracted to Methodism's early anti-slavery message, its emphasis on lay leadership, and its exuberant and participatory styles of worship, which resonated with African religious impulses. From the 1790s to about 1820, blacks comprised about twenty percent of the membership of the ME Church. The first black preacher ordained a deacon in America was Richard Allen, in 1799, at the hands of Francis Asbury. Another prominent early leader was "Black Harry" Hosier who, despite being illiterate, was a powerful and eloquent speaker, whom Bishop Thomas Coke described as "one of the best preachers in the world."[15]

Despite their presence in large numbers from the earliest days, black preachers were only allowed the status of "local preacher" (even if ordained), and not permitted to join annual conferences as itinerants with all the rights and privileges of clergy. In the early 19th century, black members began leaving the ME Church to form new denominations which provided them full ordination as clergy, and opportunities to serve as presiding elders, bishops and denominational officials. The first, the African Methodist Episcopal (AME) Church, was founded in 1818 in Philadelphia by Richard Allen, its first bishop.

Significant numbers of African Americans remained in the ME Church, however, especially in the South, where legal restrictions made it difficult for the new denominations to become planted. In the wake of the north-south split of 1844, pressure began building within the Methodist Episcopal Church to raise the status of black preachers within the church. Put simply, the ME Church was in danger of losing its black members. By 1856, delegates were ready to act, and added a paragraph to the *Discipline*, "Of the Rights and Privileges of our Colored Members," affirming the full and equal privileges of black members in quarterly conference meetings, which was the basic administrative unit for local churches. They also reaffirmed the authorization for gatherings of black lay preachers, passed four years before.[16]

This time, just such a convention was held, presided over by none other than Bishop Levi Scott. On August 5, 1857, he convened a "Conference of Colored Local Preachers," in Philadelphia's Zoar ME Church. Nineteen black preachers were present for the two-day conference, hailing from eastern Pennsylvania, New Jersey, Delaware and the Eastern Shore of Maryland and Virginia. Also present were six white presiding elders from the Philadelphia and New Jersey Conferences. On the second day, Scott was called upon to rule whether the convention had authority to elect men to deacon's and elder's orders. Scott ruled that it did not, as "the General Conference had conferred no such power, and that election to orders would be attended to by the Annual Conferences as heretofore."

Save ordination, the assembly had all the hallmarks of an annual conference session: the appointment of officers, including a secretary to keep an official journal of proceedings; committee reports; worship and preaching; establishment of a course of study for preachers under appointment; and a directive that an annual collection be taken to support needy and ailing preachers. "The greatest harmony and good feeling prevailed," Scott reported to the *Christian Advocate*; he also included in his letter to the denominational paper a list of the

An 1884 image of the original Zoar ME Church on Fourth Street,
Philadelphia, where in 1857 Scott convened the first Convention
of Colored Local Preachers (*Library Company of Philadelphia*).

---

appointments of the all preachers to their circuits, as with any
other conference session.[17] Six more such conferences would be
held annually through 1863, all under the care of Bishop Scott,
and either presided over by him, or delegated to another
minister in his stead.

Years later, several African American preachers wrote
that Scott had organized and assembled the conferences in the
face of "vigorous objections offered by the leading men of the
church."[18] These conferences represented a step forward for
black preachers within the Methodist Episcopal Church.
However, they still did not allow for full conference membership
and clergy status. That step would come sooner than most
imagined possible, but only amid the massive changes brought
on by the Civil War; and once again, Bishop Scott would play a
leading role.

An engraving of Bishop Levi Scott.

6

War Bishop

By January 1861, the American Union was coming apart. The election of Abraham Lincoln the previous November was regarded by southerners as a threat to an economic system based on unfree labor. South Carolina had passed an ordinance of secession in December, paving the way for the ten other states that would soon coalesce as the Confederate States of America. Even as various national leaders attempted compromise, and many predicted a bloodless division (or reconciliation) of the nation, Bishop Scott's assessment was more sober and realistic. In a letter to his friend Henry Slicer in January, Scott wrote:

> Our loved and boasted Union is no more! I cannot realize it, but it is in my judgment true. Compromises would avail almost nothing. The South do[es] not want compromises [and] would laugh at the North if she should make them, and the North is not likely to make them. So here we are. A Southern Confederacy or war, or a Southern Confederacy and war. Either way, war in my judgment is inevitable. The only rest I can find for the sole of my foot is just here: "The Lord reigneth" and the "wrath of man shall praise him."[1]

In the Methodist Episcopal Church, the same centrifugal forces threatened to divide the denomination for a second time in less than twenty years. The focus of the controversy within the church was the so-called "New Chapter" on slavery, added to the *Book of Discipline* at the General Conference held in Buffalo, New York in May 1860. The General Rules of the Methodist Episcopal Church had, since 1784, prohibited "the buying or selling the bodies and souls of men, women or children, with an intention to enslave them," but it did not mention "mere" ownership. This omission allowed both members and preachers to remain in good standing with the church, if they inherited slaves, or bought them before being converted, or purchased them to rescue them from a cruel master. Anti-slavery activists petitioned the General Conference of 1860 to amend the rules to prohibit "holding" slaves, which might subject slave owners in border areas like Maryland's Eastern Shore to disciplinary action. Abolitionist delegates were not able to muster quite enough votes to change the General Rule itself (which required a supermajority), but they did persuade a simple majority to add a paragraph which became known as the "New Chapter" on slavery:

> We believe that the buying, selling, or holding of human beings, to be used as chattels, is contrary to the laws of God and nature, and is inconsistent with the Golden Rule and with that Rule in our *Discipline* which requires all who desire to continue among us to "do no harm," and to "avoid evil of every kind." We therefore affectionately admonish all our Preachers and People to keep themselves pure from this great evil, and to seek its extirpation by all lawful and Christian means.[2]

There was an immediate reaction from the border conferences in Pennsylvania, Maryland, Western Virginia, Kentucky and Missouri. Fearing the new language meant a change in the terms of membership, and could result in disciplinary action or even church trials of slave-owning members, churches and circuits passed resolutions of protest, and prepared petitions to their upcoming conference sessions. They demanded the repeal of the New Chapter, and threatened to secede from the church if the new language was retained. For their part, the bishops sought to reassure members in the border conferences that the new language was pedagogical and advisory, not juridical, in nature. Scott's own views, published in the *Christian Advocate* that spring, stated flatly, "the New Chapter... has *no administrative force as law*" (emphasis original). However, Scott also made it clear that the language was intended to guide the church forward: "The substituted chapter... proclaims the belief, doctrine or sentiment of the Church... [which], taken in connection with the following affectionate admonition, as also with its position in the *Discipline*, cannot fail to have great effect. The nature and extent of that effect time alone can reveal."[3]

For now, however, the effect was to further divide the Methodist Episcopal Church. By the time the Philadelphia Conference convened for its March 1861 session, more than a thousand members on its southernmost district had withdrawn their membership, and all its churches below the Virginia State line had seceded to set up an independent "convention."[4] But all eyes were on the Baltimore Conference, which included territory in northern Virginia, and which seemed poised to vote itself out of the Methodist Episcopal Church *en masse*. It fell to Bishop Scott to superintend the annual conference session, which opened on March 13, 1861 in Staunton, Virginia.

On the first day, petitions of protest were presented, including one from a laymen's convention held the previous December declaring that Baltimore could no longer remain under the jurisdiction of the General Conference. Regular business began the next day. As recalled years later by Rev. S. V. Leech, then a young member of the body, "On Thursday at 10 AM, amid intense emotion and profound silence, the preachers turn on the brown-haired, unruffled Bishop their batteries of legal interrogatories for response." For two days, members submitted one question of church law after another to Bishop Scott, to clarify the meaning and implications of the New Chapter for the life of the conference. Scott's answers were consistent with his interpretation that nothing had changed regarding the rules on membership or ordination.[5]

Staunton, Virginia, from an 1857 engraving.

On the following Wednesday, however, Scott refused to ordain a young man named E. F. Heterick who said that his willingness to take on vows of ordination would not include submission to the New Chapter. Scott ruled that he could not ordain anyone who took their vows "with protest or exception, whether that protest or exception refers to the New Chapter or any other Chapter of the *Discipline*." The major challenge came on Saturday, March 23, amid great emotion, with "Virginia state flags... waving over the hotels and many private residences," as Rev. Leech remembered the scene. "Political and ecclesiastical excitement... [was] at white heat at Staunton." A resolution was presented protesting the New Chapter, and severing relations between the Baltimore Conference and the ME Church. Bishop Scott refused to put the matter to a vote, or to adjourn the session to allow it to meet as a "convention" to endorse the petition. The secretary of the conference, John S. Martin, called for a vote anyway. The measure passed overwhelmingly, after which Bishop Scott declared,

> The whole action just had on what is called Rev. N. Wilson's proposition, is, in my judgment, in violation of the order and *Discipline* of the ME Church, and, therefore, is null and void regarded as Conference action. I therefore do not recognize said action as infracting the integrity of this body, and so I proceed to finish the business of the present session.[6]

He did just that, completing all business, reading the preachers' appointments for the coming year, and adjourning the body on Monday, March 25. Despite the contentious nature of the session, delegates passed a resolution of thanks to Scott for "the ability, impartiality and kindness with which he has presided over our deliberations, during the embarrassments of the present session." During the next year, sixty six clergy members and most of the churches in northern Virginia withdrew from the Baltimore conference, and its membership numbers dropped from 43,581 in 1861 to just 18,679 in 1862.[7]

In a letter sent shortly afterward to his friend Henry Slicer, who was present at the conference, Scott offered his own assessment of the episode. "The Baltimore Conference on the back view seems... an instance [that]... will stand in history when fact was stranger than fiction. It has no parallel in the past; the future only can reveal whether it will have its like [again]." Nonetheless, the bishop reported with gratitude, "the singular kindness with which I was treated both by the members of the body and by the citizens of Staunton, who yet generally I believe sympathized strongly with those who desired immediate separation." He then mused darkly, "I cannot bear the thought that the ploughshare of confusion and war should be driven through the fair fields of the Baltimore Conference and of the Border."[8] Less than two weeks later, with the Confederate bombardment of Fort Sumter, the war came. The town of Staunton would suffer greatly during the war, and be burned by Union troops in 1864.

Wartime Bishop

With the outbreak of hostilities, the bishops, along with the great mass of the lay and clergy of the northern church, were swept up in the ensuing tide of indignation, patriotism, and war fever. Though his biographer maintained that Scott was among the "calmest, boldest and firmest supporters of the govern-ment... [and] a great admirer of Abraham Lincoln," his public support of the war effort was more muted than that of his colleagues, especially Bishops Simpson and Ames. Perhaps due in part to his southern roots, the bishop appears to have more anguished over the bloodletting, and far less optimistic than many at this early period for a speedy end to the conflict. "I cannot but think that the North and the South are moving under a mutual mistake," he wrote in May 1861. "Neither appreciates the other at its full value for purpose, valor, [and] resources. The future looks very dark to me – full of confusion, suffering [and] blood."[9]

Scott also was worried about his family, back in Wilmington alone as he traveled the country. In early May 1861, he received a letter from his daughter Cornelia, in which she described a rumored threat by southern agents to burn the city. "There are sixty or seventy men and two good cannon on the railroad bridge coming from Philadelphia," she reported, and went on to describe soldiers drilling, and the streets of Wilmington lined with flags, looking "very starry and striped." Then, perhaps realizing she might be causing her father anxiety, added, "Don't be alarmed about us for we are not a particle frightened."[10] In 1862, Scott moved his family and his episcopal residence to the family homestead in Odessa, where he would remain for the rest of his life.

Scott was also not enthusiastic about a policy instituted by Ames and Simpson capitalizing on Union army advances to reassert the Methodist Episcopal Church's position in the South. By 1863, the war had devastated the southern branch of Methodism. As Union troops occupied ever larger portions of southern territory, many congregations of the ME Church, South scattered, its clergy either serving with the Confederate Army or in self-imposed exile. Church buildings in many places lay empty, or were used as barracks or hospitals by the army. For many leaders of the northern church who had never accepted the legitimacy of the 1844 split, the advance of Union armies was an opportunity to re-establish a presence in the South. As Matthew Simpson put it, "There is no such Church as the Methodist Church, North. Ours is the Methodist Episcopal Church. We are not sectional." The South, therefore, was a legitimate mission field, and its abandoned churches fair game for the bishops to seek to reclaim.[11]

In 1863, Bishop Edward Ames met with Lincoln's Secretary of War, Edwin M. Stanton, to enlist the aid of military

Left: Bishop E. R. Ames. Right: Secretary of War Edwin M. Stanton.

----

authorities. Ames managed to obtain an order directing generals in the departments of Missouri, Tennessee, and the Gulf to turn over to Ames "all houses of worship belonging to the Methodist Episcopal Church, South in which a loyal minister, who has been appointed by a loyal bishop of said church... does not officiate." Before the end of the year, similar orders were issued in other military departments on behalf of Bishops Janes and Simpson, and by war's end several dozen northern preachers were under appointment to mission churches in the South.[12] Few other acts did more to embitter relations between the two branches of episcopal Methodism. Not all members of the northern church, however, were in favor of the seizures, among them Bishop Scott. In a letter to Bishop Simpson about mission efforts in the Norfolk and Portsmouth, Virginia area, Scott indicated his disapproval of seizing southern churches. "We might by aid of [the] military take the church," he wrote, "but I can have no part in that policy."[13]

Although he opposed using military authorities as allies, Bishop Scott nonetheless supported the establishment of mission churches and conferences in the South, especially among the newly freed slaves. The 1864 General Conference, held in Scott's old pastoral charge, Union Church, Philadelphia, empowered the bishops "when in their judgement they deem it expedient... to organize a conference or conferences in the southern states and in the territories."[14] The conference also allocated funds for the mission to the South, and elected three new bishops to help manage its expanded territorial ambitions: Edward Thomson, Calvin Kingsley and Davis W. Clark.

The first to be created was the Holston Conference, established in Tennessee in June 1865 by Bishop Clark. This was followed by the Mississippi Mission Conference, organized by Bishop Thomson in December 1865; the South Carolina Mission Conference by Bishop Baker in April 1866; and the Tennessee Conference by Bishop Clark six months later. In December 1866, in Portsmouth, Virginia, Levi Scott organized the Virginia and North Carolina Conference with just fourteen elders, the fifth southern mission conference established in the subjugated South by the ME Church. Scott was recalled to have remarked at the close of the founding session, "I have organized several conferences, but I never organized one so small that I didn't know what to do with it when I was done."[15] By the time the 1868 General Conference convened, nine such mission conferences had been created in the South. Notably, these bodies were integrated, served by both black and white preachers and presiding elders.[16]

Clergy Status for Americans

With the excitements and dislocations caused by the war, the internal debate over slavery, race and the status of blacks within the Methodist Episcopal Church faded into the background for a time. With the advance of the armies, however, and especially with the advent of emancipation in 1863, pressure increased to extend full clergy status to black preachers. When the quadrennial General Conference convened in Philadelphia in May 1864, a major focus of its deliberations was outreach and ministry among African Americans, both the newly freed slaves of the South, and the free blacks of the north.

Ministers of the Mississippi Mission Conference, showing
black and white preachers in the same body, in an 1866
engraving which appeared in *Harper's Weekly.* Bishop
Edward Thomson is seated in the low chair at the center.

The body finally amended the General Rules to prohibit
slaveholding, as well as the buying and selling of slaves,
something the abolitionist wing had pursued for years. It also
created a "Committee on the State of the Work Among People of
Color," which recommended that "the bishops be... authorized
to organize among our colored ministers, for the benefit of our
colored members and population, Mission Conferences – one or
more – where in their godly judgement the exigencies of the
work may demand it." The plan was approved by delegates, who
also created and outlined the boundaries of the first two: the
Washington Conference, covering "Western Maryland, the
District of Columbia, Virginia, and the territory south;" and the
Delaware Conference, taking in the area "north and west of the
Washington Conference."[7] The first to be established was the
Delaware Conference, which met for its founding session in
Philadelphia, July 28-31, 1864, under the leadership of Bishop
Edmund S. Janes, assisted by Bishop Simpson. For the first time
in the United States, black preachers were ordained, made full
members of an annual conference of the Methodist Episcopal

Church, and appointed to serve as presiding elders. Though
Bishop Scott was not part of the proceedings, the Delaware
Conference was built directly upon the structures and
procedures he had established during his supervision of the
previous seven annual sessions of the Conferences of Colored
Local Preachers.[18]

Scott undoubtedly would have been present but for
another bout of debilitating illness. In a letter to Rev. N. J. B.
Morgan of Baltimore dated July 30, he wrote that he had been
"very sick – am convalescing, but feeble." Nonetheless, the
formation of the new conferences was very much on his mind,
and he told Morgan of his intention to open the Washington
Conference in Baltimore in late October.[19] The situation in
Maryland was different than that of Pennsylvania, which had
long been a free state. Since Maryland had remained loyal to the
Union, its slaves had not been freed by Lincoln's Emancipation
Proclamation, which applied only to territory controlled by the
Confederacy. Nevertheless, under pressure from the Lincoln Administration, Maryland political leaders saw the handwriting on
the wall, and in 1864 adopted a new constitution that abolished
the "peculiar institution," to take effect on November 1 that year.

On October 27, Bishop Scott convened the first session
of the Washington Conference, in Baltimore's Sharp Street ME
Church. For the first time in a slave state, black preachers were
welcomed into full membership in an annual conference, and
ordained deacons and elders with full rights as clergy members
of the Methodist Episcopal Church. On October 30 and 31, Scott
ordained four deacons and two elders, and at the session's close,
read the appointments for the coming year, which included two
black presiding elders: Benjamin Brown, assigned to oversee
twelve pastoral charges on the Chesapeake District; and James
H. Harper, superintending nine more on the Potomac District.[20]

Deeply aware of the historic nature of the event, Bishop
Scott addressed the body at the close of the session on October
31, a synopsis of which was recorded by the secretary, Benjamin
Brown. Scott began by noting how, "for the first time, they [the
African Americans of Maryland] had exercised the function of a
conference, ...elected men to orders, and admitted preachers on
trial and had, in their midst, the first transferred colored

Sharp Street ME Church Baltimore, built in 1860. Here Bishop
Scott founded the Washington Conference in 1864.

---

preacher... The beginning of a conference, it is true, is small, but
who can tell what, by the blessing of God, it may become?" He
then went on to reflect on the fact that the new state
constitution would take effect on the same day the body would
disperse to fan out across the state to proclaim the glad tidings
of salvation:

> [T]he day on which the first Annual Conference of Colored
> Preachers of the Methodist Episcopal Church, ever held in
> the state of Maryland, closes, is the day on which the
> dominion of slavery ceases. Ninety thousand of your
> brethren... will lie down tonight – if indeed they do lie down
> – with the Manacles of Slavery upon them; but when the
> midnight hour shall strike, even as the angel came and
> unloosed Peter, and he arose a free man, so shall their chains
> fall off, and these thousands shall rise to the dignity of free
> men.[21]

An engraving showing the bishops of the Methodist Episcopal
Church in 1864. Standing, left to right: Edward R. Ames,
Matthew Simpson, Edmund S. Janes, Levi Scott,
Edward Thomson. Sitting, left to right: Calvin Kingsley,
Thomas A. Morris, Osmon C. Baker, Davis W. Clark.

Scott then encouraged the assembled delegates "to prove
to the world their capacity for self-government, and their
worthiness of the great boon which God had so mercifully
granted them." For their part, conference members passed
resolutions thanking Scott for "the ability and impartiality with
which he has presided over our deliberations," and exulting in
their new status as free people:

> [W]e do hereby offer devout thanksgiving and praise to the
> Giver of all good, for the blessings of His Providence in
> making Maryland a Free State, and restoring to liberty many
> of our brethren, who have heretofore been in bondage. To
> God be the glory, and to us, the privilege and duty of making
> this dispensation available for our moral and intellectual
> elevation.[22]

While the Delaware and Washington Conferences
brought full ordination and conference membership for black

preachers, they were still segregated by race, and under the supervision of white bishops. Not all were in favor of this approach. Rev. Gilbert Haven of New England (later a bishop), for example, argued against separate conferences in favor of full integration, and called for rejecting any "doctrine of caste" within the church.[23] To Bishop Scott and many others, however, it was a matter of advancing principle in a pragmatic manner. In the face of deep-seated societal racism, many believed it impossible to integrate black and white preachers within the existing structures of the church. Black preachers serving black congregations would be the most effective and fruitful way to retain and serve its black membership. Segregated conferences, they thought, was the only way to provide full clergy status for blacks in a communion where many of its clergy and laity, especially in the border conferences, were not yet willing to accept it.

While Scott's approach elevated the status of African Americans within the church, it did, in the end, have the effect of institutionalizing segregation, and delaying for a century a fully integrated denomination. In fact, the precedent of the Washington and Delaware Conferences was used to introduce segregation among the southern mission conferences, which initially had been composed of black and white preachers serving in the same bodies.[24]

7

Senior Bishop

In the years after the war, Scott continued to suffer from periodic episodes of confinement due to poor health, but remained remarkably active nonetheless. His responsibilities, in fact, increased, as the number of southern mission conferences grew, and especially after the deaths of four of his episcopal colleagues in 1870 and 1871, reducing the number of effective bishops to just four. In 1871, at age 69, Bishop Scott was responsible to superintend sixteen annual conference sessions all around the country. Relief came at the General Conference of 1872, which elected eight new bishops to lead the church.[1]

The year 1871 brought another sorrow into the lives of Levi and Sarah Scott: the death of their daughter, Emma, wife of Rev. James Mitchell, in Leesburg, Virginia – the fifth of their seven children to predecease them. "I appreciate your distressing loneliness," Levi wrote his bereaved son-in-law. "Emma will not return. O for the faith that overcomes the world!"[2]

During this period, Bishop Scott continued to support the development of the ME Church's newly established conferences for its black constituency. He presided over the Washington Conference just one more time after its founding session, in 1866. But in a letter to Bishop Simpson in February 1867, Scott wrote, "I organized on Christmas Day the Centenary Biblical Institute in Balt[imore] for the education of col[ore]d ministers."[3] The new school, which would supply trained clergy to the Washington Conference for many years, opened its doors in January 1867 with twenty students, under the instruction of two conference ministers, Revs. James H. Brown and William Hardin. In 1875, the school began admitting women, and expanded its mission to train teachers. This is the origin of today's Morgan State University, the largest historically black university in Maryland.[4]

Scott remained even more closely connected to the Delaware Conference, presiding over its annual sessions in 1865, 1870, 1871, 1872, 1877 and 1879. That last year, Scott and the black preachers met July 24-28, in the Waugh Methodist Episcopal Church, in Cambridge, Maryland, once a center of the slave trade on the Eastern Shore, and the hometown of Harriet Tubman. Aware that it was likely his last time to lead their deliberations, Scott mused on his history with the body:

> If I am not a father to any other conference, I am to this one. I called your local preachers together from '57 to '64, and met them every year but one... When you met first as an annual conference you had some experience. I thank God for the progress you have made, and rejoice at your record... I am not ashamed to be known as the father of this conference. I am glad to know that you have real, earnest business men here, and [that] buncombe, spread-eagle speeches are not now the order of the day... The principle under which our early Methodism lived and grew was what might vulgarly be styled the "Root hog or die" principle. I am glad you have rooted yourselves to the soil and commenced to grow... [A]s I swing around the circle... I find improvement everywhere.
>
> >   Praise God from whom all blessing flow!
> >   Praise him all creatures here below![5]

Left: Rev. Nathan Young, one of the black preachers Levi Scott organized in the late 1850s, and who led public prayers with the bishop at the 1879 Delaware Conference session. Young later co-authored a tribute to Scott after the bishop's death. Right: Rev. John G. Manluff, another founding member of the Delaware Conference who had his start under Scott's leadership in the 1850s, and who died earlier in 1879; Bishop Scott spoke in tribute to Manluff during the conference memorial service that year.

For their part, the preachers passed a resolution of thanks to Scott, calling him their "esteemed and much beloved bishop," and commending the way in which he "presided with care and judgment over us while in session." They ended their statement with the prayer that God would "keep him through life, and in the end translate him among the leaders of the church and the redeemed in the kingdom of eternal bliss." The delegates also passed a resolution calling upon the upcoming General Conference of 1880 to elect a black bishop for service in the United States. "We believe the time has arrived for the election of a man of African descent to the office of bishop in the ME Church," the petition read, "[and] we instruct our delegates to use all lawful means to accomplish the aforesaid end."[6]

An engraving from *Harper's Weekly* of the 1868 General
Conference of the ME Church, held in Chicago. It was among
the duties of Scott and the other bishops to preside at these
sessions, which were held once every four years, and which
functioned as the governing body of the entire denomination.

Senior Bishop

In 1876, Bishop Edmund S. Janes died, and Levi Scott
became the senior bishop of the Methodist Episcopal Church.
That same year, he presided over the annual session of the
Wilmington Conference, which had been formed in 1868, when
the General Conference detached the Delmarva Peninsula from
the Philadelphia Conference. Back home and among friends,
some of whom he had known for more than half a century, Scott
was asked to deliver a sermon in recognition of the fiftieth
anniversary of his entering the itinerant ministry. His message of
March 20 was less a sermon than a collection of reminiscences.
He spoke of the remarkable growth of Methodism in numbers,
wealth, and influence, painted character sketches of colorful
preachers of the past, described the struggle over slavery, and
reflected on his mortality:

The generation of Methodist preachers of 1826 is now nearly all passed away, and the few who remain give unmistakable attestations of the great fact so beautifully formulated by Isaiah, "We all do fade away as a leaf..." And now... [we] stand... on the bald, bleak bluff of the cold river. Yet thanks be to God who gives us the victory though our Lord Jesus Christ! We do not dread its chilling waves... May the admonition of our Lord, "Be ye also ready, for in such an hour as ye think not, the Son of Man cometh," be ever sounding in our ears until our work is done and we are safe at home.[7]

Whenever home in Odessa, Scott continued to attend the church of his childhood, and to lend his support for its ministry and maintenance. In 1877, Union was remodeled, and in December was rededicated with special services Scott helped to lead. "Sabbath at Union was a very successful day," he wrote Bishop Simpson on December 6. "The balance of the money need to pay the entire debt incurred was raised in the morning and afternoon without begging, and the evening collection was for ordinary purposes. The congregations were large. There were five forward for prayer on Sunday night. The reopening services will ever be remembered by those who were present."[8]

Tour of the South

In 1878, all of Bishop Scott's assigned conferences were in the South. In December 1877, the 75-year old senior bishop embarked by rail, arriving in Charleston, South Carolina where he preached December 30 at the Centenary ME Church, a large black congregation. Accompanied by his widowed son-in-law James Mitchell, Scott made his way to Savannah, Georgia for a brief stay; then to Florida, with stops in St. Augustine and Jacksonville, before arriving in Gainesville to convene the Florida Conference on January 9. From there he traveled to Columbia, South Carolina to preside over the South Carolina Conference, January 16-21; then to North Carolina for another conference session in Lumberton the following week. His last conferences were held in the fall season, when he superintended the Holston, Tennessee, and East Tennessee Conferences.[9]

Two bishops of the ME Church, South, whom Scott invited to
preach during conference sessions of the northern ME Church.
Left: Bishop Hubbard H. Kavanaugh. Right: Bishop J.T. Wightman.

Aware this was probably his final tour of the South,
Scott's public utterances were tinged with nostalgia, reminiscing
about earlier visits, and relating stories from his early life and
conversion. In Florida he said, "I meet you for the first time,
[and] possibly the last... I am now admonished that my days are
drawing to a close, yet I am not distressed thereby; the outlook
is calm, bright and beautiful." In Tennessee he addressed the
class of deacons, saying, "Do you remember a wonderful feeling
in your heart of a change? I never put this question but I look
back to the period when I was converted. There it stands as a
monument in my past history. Though I have had clouds, yet I
have never brought a reproach on the Christian name. And now,
my brethren, I trust you will look forward to the things that are
before."[10]

He expressed his concerns about the spirituality of the
church in his day. While celebrating the advances made by
Methodists in education, culture, and church architecture, he
fretted over the depth of Christian experience among the rising

generation of clergy. "Mr. Wesley regarded personal piety as the fundamental qualification for the Christian ministry," he reminded delegates at the Tennessee Conference. "You may have culture – we can never discredit culture – but we esteem personal piety as the fundamental qualification." Later in the same session he exhorted them to "go on to perfection [as]... the law of the spiritual life... It is essential to our usefulness, not only as ministers, but as Christians. God grant to you a continued growth... O let us go on to perfection!"[11]

Scott also made conciliatory gestures to leaders of the Methodist Episcopal Church, South. It was not new with him. As far back as 1856, while presiding over the California Conference, Scott had invited southern Bishop H. H. Kavanaugh to sit beside him on the dais, and to preach to the assembly. In 1870 he had signed a public letter to the leaders of the southern church calling for a reunification of the divided branches of American Methodism. In January 1878, at the Florida Conference session, Scott invited southern Methodist preacher Rev. John P. Duncan, Chaplain of the Georgia Senate, to address the delegates; and while presiding over the North Carolina Conference, he invited southern Bishop J. T. Wightman to preach.[12]

Last Years

1879 turned out to be Levi Scott's last year in effective service as bishop. He presided over conference sessions in Kentucky, North Indiana, Maryland, Alabama and Savannah, Georgia. In the fall of that year, his wife Sarah fell dangerously ill – she had been in poor health for decades – and Scott suspended plans to superintend the Georgia Conference, to care for his wife. She died on November 25, 1879, three days after the couple's 49th wedding anniversary. Scott was so stricken by the loss that he was unable to attend her funeral at Union Church. Instead, a brief service was held with him at his home, led by Scott's close friend, Rev. Lucius Matlack, and Bishop Simpson. Matlack remained with Scott as the procession went to the church for the formal funeral, led by Simpson and seven other ministers.[13] Scott was devastated by Sarah's death. A few weeks later, he wrote his son-in-law,

I still sleep in the library. Mother's room has been put in order for me. I expect to go to it tonight, even though everything in it seems to have a voice and to be a reminder of the wife of my youth, the mother of my children... [and] faithful companion of my varied life for more than forty-nine years, now absent, never to return. We can endure the absence of a friend, even though on the other side of the globe, when we have a reasonable hope that that friend will return some day. But my friend is absent, not in some place on this planet, but in another world. Absent from the body, from the family, from me; but present with her parents, with her precious Emma, and the children, and, best of all, with the Lord, to return hither never, never.[14]

Sarah's passing seemed to sap Levi of his remaining strength. Though assigned to superintend the New Jersey and East German Conferences in the spring of 1880, he was unable to do so. In April, he wrote to Bishop Simpson, "I have failed in all my work since the death of Mrs. Scott. I was at the New Jersey Conf[erence] as you know, but did nothing except ordain a Deacon... I failed entirely to go to East German Conference... I have been confined almost entirely to the house for the last 10 days, with severe neuralgia in my left eye and head, and am in doubt as to my future course." The next month, the bishops were to assemble in preparation for the 1880 General Conference, to be held in Cincinnati, and Scott added, "I wish to be at General Conference and at our meeting the Wednesday before. But I am in great doubt."[15]

He somehow mustered the strength to travel to the quadrennial gathering in May, but was too sick to participate actively in much of the business of the conference. At the first meeting of the board of bishops after the election of four new episcopal leaders (Henry W. Warren, Cyrus D. Foss, John F. Hurst and Gilbert Haven), Levi Scott announced his retirement, and expressed his confidence in the future of his beloved church. It was recalled that he "spoke a loving word" to each of his episcopal colleagues, and said "I go into retirement with a cheerful spirit... In such hands, the Church is safe."[16]

Above: detail from an 1881 map of New Castle County, showing
The location of Bishop Scott's home (just right of center, at
bottom). Below: a photograph of Bishop Scott's home,
"Itinerant's Lodge," from an article in the *Christian Advocate*
of October 9, 1902. The building no longer stands.

Left: Scott's friend, Rev. Lucius Matlack. Right: Dr. Ellwood
Stokes, who wrote of a visit to the bishop in 1880.

During the train journey back home, accompanied by
his son-in-law, James Mitchell, Scott suffered a stroke which
paralyzed his left arm. He never fully recovered. Levi Scott spent
the remainder of his days in Odessa, living in the family homestead with his daughter, Cornelia Townsend, and her family.
Scott corresponded with friends and colleagues, and received
visitors in his home, which he dubbed "Itinerant's Lodge."

He kept his sense of humor, which came through in a
letter he sent to the General Missionary Committee, which met
in New York just after the 1880 presidential election. *The New
York Times* reported that the letter of the "aged and humorously
inclined Bishop" was read to the group "amid much merriment."
Scott expressed his satisfaction at the Republican victory,
bending Psalm 49 a bit: "The Lord Reigneth. Let the people
(Demo[crats]s) tremble;" adding, "My native state is detaching
herself from the solid South." The *Times* reported that "even the
Democrats present smiled at the good Bishop's enthusiasm."[7]

Among the visitors who came to see Scott in retirement
was Dr. Ellwood Stokes, president of the Ocean Grove (New
Jersey) Camp Meeting Association, in November 1880. He was

greeted at the bishop's door by Rev. Matlack and welcomed by the bishop with a "genial smile and kindly words." He found Scott "pleasantly situated," well-cared for by his daughter and son-in-law, and enjoying the company of his eight week-old twin grandchildren. Stokes went on to describe Scott's condition:

> I found the bishop better than I expected. True, he carries his left arm in a sling, which from paralysis is swollen and useless. The whole of his left side, particularly his left foot, sympathizes with this condition, and although he walks about the house, and when the weather is fair, around the yard and garden; yet his movements are slow, tottering, and much inconvenienced by his late attack. His sight is much impaired, so that he reads with much difficulty, and but little at a time. Nevertheless, his autograph, which he gave me, is clear, bold and strong; almost, if not quite equal, to what it was in his best days. His face is full – fuller than I ever remember to have seen it – and although his beard, which from his inability to shave has been allowed to grow, changes his appearance somewhat. His mind is clear, his memory good, his heart warm, and when drawn out in conversation, he fires up with the old magnetic fervor which thrills from head to foot. We sat and talked about the olden days until after 10 o'clock – more than an hour after the bishop's bedtime; "and yet," said he, "I might as well sit up till 12 or 1, or 2 o'clock, for I never sleep until toward morning." He retired to his room, and Dr. Matlack and I to ours, but not to sleep, until many a scene of the past had been talked over and re-enjoyed.[18]

Scott continued to attend worship as often as his health allowed, though more often at St. Paul's Church nearer his home, than at Union. He often sat on a chair reserved for him within the chancel, where he could be seen listening attentively to the message and deeply engaged in the worship. It was recalled that "as he tottered down the aisle after service, numbers tarried to clasp hands with him," seeking a blessing from a man many locals regarded as a home-grown saint. "Well, sister," he remarked to another elderly worshipper one day, "we are lingering here yet; the dear ones have gone ahead of us. We

The interior of St. Paul's ME Church, Odessa, where
Bishop Scott often worshipped in his later years.

----

have difficulty in getting here; we can scarcely climb the stairs.
Never mind, we'll take wings after a while, and get along better,
and sing with the angels in the upper sanctuary."[19]

In March 1882, the Wilmington Conference met for its
annual session in Middetown, Delaware, less than four miles
from the Scott homestead. Rev. Robert W. Todd led a small
delegation to visit with the infirm bishop, and present him with
a ceremonial cane made from wood taken from Barratt's Chapel,
where Scott had preached in the 1820s. "I have come today to
give you a good caning," Rev. Todd teased the bishop in his
formal presentation. "You once laid hands on me; and why
should I not, now that I have a good opportunity, retaliate?" A
silver band on the cane was inscribed "to the Senior Bishop,"
and, as Todd explained, "when you shall at last go up to possess
the land where patriarchs get young again and where pilgrims
have wings, you will leave it as a legacy to the next Senior in
office."[20]

An image of Levi Scott's daughter Cornelia, and her husband, George Townsend, with whom the bishop lived in his last years. George Townsend later became a state representative, a customs official and a US Marshall. The image, based on an old photo, was drawn by artist Brian Lehman of Lancaster County, Pennsylvania.

That day came sooner than perhaps any in the room expected. Bishop Levi Scott died at his home on the morning of July 13, 1882. His last words reportedly were, "Come, Lord Jesus, come quickly." His funeral was held four days later at Union ME Church, led by Bishops Matthew Simpson and Edward G. Andrews. Among the participants were the bishop's son, Rev. Alfred T. Scott, and his colleague and friend from the early days of ministry in Philadelphia, Rev. Anthony Atwood. In attendance were preachers and dignitaries, including a former governor of Delaware, John P. Cochran. Statements were read on behalf of the Preachers' Meetings of Philadelphia and New York City. But most noteworthy was "the outpouring of personal affection from his neighbors, almost unparalleled in the history of public men," as a participant recalled. "Nowhere is his fame so jealously guarded, his character so revered, as in that circle that saw him when all the restraints of official dignity were unfelt."[21]

The principal address was delivered by Bishop Matthew Simpson, with whom Scott had been elected to the episcopacy thirty years before. Simpson paid tribute to the quiet, steady leadership of his colleague, especially during the turmoil of the 1850s and 1860s, calling Scott "a wise, careful, and judicious overseer of God's Church." Simpson also devoted a significant

Bishop Matthew Simpson, with whom Scott had been
elected to the episcopacy in 1852, and who spoke
at the funeral (*Simpson House, Philadelphia*).

portion of his tribute to Scott's role in the education and uplift
of African Americans in the church and beyond, declaring that
Bishop Scott "had wide views and a loving heart."[22] He was laid
to rest beside his beloved Sarah in the cemetery of the church
where he had first worshipped as a child. A marble obelisk
marks the spot where Levi Scott awaits the last trumpet call.

Tributes poured in from around the country. A notice in
the *New York Times* described the Bishop's performance of his
duties as "long and honorably adorned by a wisdom and purity
which the Church has never questioned."[23] In a tribute which
appeared in the *Philadelphia Methodist*, Rev. J. B. McCullough
said of Scott, "As a companion in travel, or in the social circle, he
was simply charming. [He was] a natural gentleman; a pure
Christian, a judicious administrator; and able minister of Jesus

Christ."[24] But perhaps the most earnest accolade came from the black members of the Delaware Conference, who met for their annual session just one week after Bishop Scott's death in Centreville, Maryland – the same town where Rev. Thomas Scott had died in 1803, after giving his dying blessing to his infant son Levi. The ministers passed a resolution written by Revs. Nathan Young, Hooper Jolly and Wesley J. Parker, declaring, "from the beginning to the end, [Levi Scott] manifested himself a friend of the colored race, especially those who were members of the Methodist Episcopal Church." The statement went on to declare,

> Bishop Scott will not be forgotten when the names of John Brown, Abraham Lincoln, General Ulysses S. Grant and General James A. Garfield are being read and thought of as the heroes of true national freedom in this county.[25]

Within that constellation of national stars, however, the memory of Levi Scott soon faded. Nevertheless, he cast a wide shadow over the Methodism of his day. An active participant in the controversies that divided the church in the 1840s, he provided steady and determined leadership to his church during the tumultuous days of the Civil War and reconstruction. He helped raise the status, standing and educational opportunities for African Americans in the church, though in a manner that had the effect of perpetuating segregation for decades. And he was a thoroughly Wesleyan, who promoted personal piety and the call to sanctification as the most important foundations for ministry and for life. A man of quiet and reserved temperament, Scott was not one to thrust himself into the limelight, nor was he easily ruffled. His leadership skills, eloquence, and sober judgment made him an effective preacher, administrator and episcopal leader for more than fifty years.

The obelisk marking the grave of Bishop Levi Scott,
in the burial ground of Old Union Church, Odessa.

Appendix A
Bishop Scott's Funeral

The following account of the funeral observances for Bishop Levi Scott appeared in the *Every Evening Wilmington Daily Commercial*, a Wilmington, Delaware newspaper, in its issues of Monday, July 17 and Tuesday, July 18, 1882. Bound copies of the paper are in the Wilmington Historical Society.

Monday, July 17, 1882

Bishop Scott's Funeral
The Clergymen Present – Arrival of the Funeral Cortege at Union Church

Odessa, July 17 – The funeral of the late Bishop Scott has drawn a very large throng to this place. The body was laid out at the bishop's late residence, robed in a plain black shroud, with a sheaf of wheat at his feet, and his features natural and life-like. He reposed in a plain walnut casket. A peculiarity was the absence of flowers.

There was a large concourse at the house, including the following ministers of the Wilmington Conference: Revs. Thomas E. Bell, James E. Bryan, William B. Gregg, Charles Hill, J. L. Houston, T. B. Hunter, William H. Hutchin, T. E. Martindale, L. C. Matlack, George W. Miller, W. L. S. Murray, T. A. H. O'Brien, C. W. Prettyman, John D. Rigg, M. A. Richards, John Shilling, Adam Stengle, T. E. Terry, J. T. VanBurkalow, and others; a committee from the trustees of Grace and Zion Churches, and Madeley Chapel; Bishops Simpson of Philadelphia and Andrews of Washington; Dr. A. J. Kynett of New York; Revs. William

Swindells, G. D. Carrow, W. J. Paxton, W. D. Kurtz, Jacob Hinson, G. W. Lybrand, J. S. J. McConnell, A. Atwood, W. L. Gray and Joseph Mason. J. F. Crouch, A. Longacre, and Andrew Manship of Philadelphia and vicinity.

The services at the house opened with singing by the Odessa Church choir, in a fine and impressive manner, the hymn beginning,

> There's a wideness in God's mercy,
> Like the wideness of the sea.

Bishop Andrews followed this by fervent prayer. At 1 PM, the remains were borne to the hearse by six of Bishop Scott's grandsons; four of them sons of Rev. A. T. Scott, and two sons of George Townsend. The funeral cortege proceeded to the Union ME Church, where an immense concourse of people viewed the remains. The Rev. William H. Hutchins, formerly pastor of the Odessa Church, who had lived with the bishop many years, opened the services at the church by reading an interesting memoir of the home life of the deceased. "Bishop Scott," said he, "is dead:"

We meet today, in common grief, to mingle our tears; to unite in extolling the virtues of the dead. The vicinity of his late residence had been familiar to him throughout his life. In a log house nearby, where the good man met his fate, he was born. He loved his home, for her old trees had records and legends; and many old houses in the vicinity are rich in marriage festivals or funeral solemnities. He walked among his neighbors with unaffected modesty. The old members, who have known him through all the grades of his growth, from the farm lad to the seniority in the bishopric of the church, offer sincere and affectionate testimony to the uniformity of his unaffected familiarity and yet grave apprehension of the duties and dignities of the elevation, which had moved to him. Everyone who knew him loved him keenly. Critical eyes scanned him closely in all of his business relations, and the church at large will accept with gladness the verdict voiced by the humblest of his fellow citizens.

Bishop Scott was a square man. No breathe of aspersion has tarnished his record as a bishop, a Christian minister, a

Union Church, Odessa, early 20th century, showing
Bishop Scott's tomb (*Delaware State Archives*).

----

man, a father, a husband. His piety, upright walk, and
chastity secured him the title, "the good Bishop and holy
man of God." His character is likened to that of the Apostle
John. I picture him as a man past three score years and ten,
to be in whose society was like standing amid a glory of light
and color. It was like breathing the odor from a thousand
pastures of fragrant flowers; like the melody of pure joy and
the harmony of perfect blessedness.

The heart is fed, the mind is satisfied, the soul is strength-
ened by such a life. Let the air breathed by our better selves
be represented with its own sublimity in colors that shall be
visible for years after the form and soul have gone home.

The churches in the vicinity were his constant solicitude.
He assisted in the administration of the Sacrament of the
Lord's Supper, until no longer able himself to bear the
emblems to the communicants, but after that sat by and
assisted at the tables, while listeners were bathed in tears.

The strength of his love for home and his family were dwelt
upon lengthily, as also was his love for his wife. The story was
told with pathos and beauty, of his carrying the picture of his

wife in his heart and saying, "Mother's before me day and night, if I am a thousand miles away from home."

> When he returned from the General Conference in 1880, he realized his work was ended, and said the conference is the grandest assemblage in the church. He said, "I come home contented, satisfied. The work has been committed into competent hands. I am content in my own case to await patiently the future developments of my Father's will." His last minutes were triumphant and his time was spent in reciting favorite passages from Scripture. In the final struggle, he uttered again and again "Come Jesus, come quickly."

The Rev. Anthony Atwood followed in an interesting address on the bishop's early life, his struggles and studies. Bishops Andrews and Simpson made brief addresses upon the work of the deceased, dwelling upon his excellent work, "devoted to duty and what accomplished." The Revs. Valentine Gray and Joseph Mason also made brief addresses. Rev. George W. Miller of Grace Church made the final prayer at the grave.

Tuesday, July 18, 1882

Dust to Dust
Funeral Services at Union ME Church
Over the Remains of Bishop Scott

The special dispatch from Odessa in *Every Evening* yesterday covered pretty fully the funeral service over the remains of Bishop Scott. Owing to the lateness of the hour, it was impossible to telegraph an entirely full account of the services at the church, which are now given as supplemental.

As the pall-bearers carrying the remains entered the church, the choir of Odessa Church chanted a sad, funereal, yet beautiful hymn, which was followed by hymn number 724 as cited by Rev. Adam Stengle. Dr. A. Longacre then offered a prayer, followed by scriptural readings by Revs. Charles Hill and John Wilson. The singing of another hymn, cited by Rev. M. A. Richards, followed.

Left: Bishop Scott's son, Rev. Alfred T. Scott. Right: Rev. Anthony Atwood, Bishop Scott's colleague and friend, who also spoke at the 1882 funeral service in Odessa.

Dr. G. D. Carrow, of the Philadelphia Committee of Methodist ministers to draft suitable resolutions upon the death of Bishop Scott, then read the following:

The Preachers' Meeting of Philadelphia and vicinity having with unfeigned sorrow heard of the death of the Rev. Levi Scott, DD, Senior Bishop of the Methodist Episcopal Church, at his home in the state of Delaware, on the 13th of July 1882, convened at the usual place of meeting for the purpose of taking such action as would properly express their sense of the excellence of his character and the value of his long and eminent service to the cause of Christ and of the bereavement they, in common with the whole church, have sustained in his removal from the scene of his great responsibilities, ordered the preparation of a suitable memorial to be entered upon their journal, and read as a part of the funeral obsequies.

While we sincerely mourn the departure of our venerated and beloved chief pastor, we thankfully recognize the watchful providence, which, through paths of care, toil and danger, protected his life to the age of four-score years; and the redeeming grace that made him what he was in the esteem of man and in the eyes of God. Divinely commissioned to preach the gospel in the morning of life, the divine virtue of the gospel found in his Christian experience and ministerial character and service a most impressive and striking exemplification. Great and precious gifts were imparted to him in the attributes of his natural constitution of mind and body. In an apparently frail physique there ushered an unusual degree of vitality; and in a clear, transparent soul existed intellectual and moral faculties which formed a solid and congenial basis for the distinction to which he attained. Only on such a natural foundation can ever be built the structure of a character so harmonious and beautiful. Nature had done so much for him that it was possible for grace to produce on him its highest consummation. Perhaps his chief endowment was the balance of his powers. There seemed to be no excess in any one faculty, and consequently none in the combined faculties acting in any one direction. His perception, to the extent of its measure, was penetrating and accurate. His judgment, to the limit of his insight, was perhaps as nearly infallible as it is possible for man's to be. With nerves extremely sensitive, his self-control was complete and almost invincible. In the soil of his moral nature grew sympathy, tenderness, simplicity, sincerity – in a word, true childlikeness. These in him were natural dispositions, and these, with others of kindred nature, were purified by the Holy Spirit, and all placed in subjection to a conscience that reigned as lord paramount over his heart and life. He was exceled in scholastics, in science, in eloquence, in knowledge of the Great World by some of his colleagues; but in purity, in self-abnegation, weight of Christian character and single-eyed devotion to Jesus Christ, by none of them, nor by any of his or their predecessors. All that concentrates in the one word goodness was accorded to him by all who ever knew him. He was one of the best of scholars among the self-educated men of his day. The list of his studies was not so long, nor the range of his reading so wide and varied as that of a few of his contemporary non-graduates, but what he knew was thoroughly mastered and never forgotten.

A recent photograph of the interior of Old Union Church,
where Bishop Scott's funeral was held.

In all the principal elements of effective preaching
Bishop Scott was a master. Not one of his contemporaries
excelled him in rendering a critically exact sense of the
Scriptures. His sermons were clear, concise, direct, pointed,
spiritual, experimental, practical always, and occasionally
moving and overwhelming. In counsel he was wise, and in
administering the economy of the church was able, impartial,
and faithful. He was a gentleman in every instinct of his
nature. In his private and public relations he was as regardful
of the proprieties as were the best types of Christian chivalry
in days of old, and was as courteous and graceful in his
bearing as though he had been bred at the first court of
Christendom. As a companion in travel or at the fireside he
was instructive, genial and charming. His sense of wit and
humor, and especially of the ludicrous, was broad and deep
and keen, but never bitter, never sarcastic, never indulged at
the expense of the ignorant or unfortunate. A volume might
be added in delineation, so much is offered, though felt to be
all inadequate, as an affectionate tribute to his memory by
his brethren and sons in the gospel who "sorrow most of all"

that in this world, "they shall see his face no more." During sixty years he gave himself wholly to the work of his ministry; and then "he was not, for God took him."

G. D. Carrow	J. M. Hinson
W. J. Paxon	G. W. Lybrand
M. S. Kurtz	A. Atwood
W. Swindells	W. G. Gray
J. S. J. McConnell	Joseph Mason

Rev. William Hutchins, who lived in the family of Bishop Scott three years and was pastor of the Odessa church, then read a paper on the home life of the deceased, as was telegraphed and appeared in the third edition of *Every Evening* yesterday.

Bishop Simpson of Philadelphia then made a most eloquent address. He referred to the General Conference of 1848, and to the one in 1852, when he and the dead bishop with a class numbering three or four others were elected to the bishopric. Bishop Scott at the election received the highest number of votes, and consequently was elected senior bishop, which right gave him preference of selecting a place of residence in the episcopate. In his remarks referring to Bishop Scott's love of the church and his devotion to church duty, Bishop Simpson said, "at the last General Conference he attended in Cincinnati in 1880, he was not able to preside over the assemblage, but sat and listened to the proceedings with unabated interest, and expressed himself of being content and satisfied with the work done by this body. He was also unable to take an active part in the ordination services, but requested that he be permitted to place his hand on the head of the ordained with the other bishops. This was the last time the speaker had ever seen the deceased bishop at a Board of Bishops meeting." He paid a glowing and eloquent tribute to the character, life and works of the deceased. He closed with the quotation: "*Weary man, cease thy wanderings; Hie thee to thy home;*" which was quoted by Bishop Scott at the closing of the General Conference in Cincinnati in 1880.

Bishop Andrews then made an eloquent address, beginning with the quotation, "*There is no death! What seems so is transition.*"

Left: Rev. Goldsmith D. Carrow, who read the statement eulogizing Bishop Scott prepared by the Methodist preachers of Philadelphia. Right: Bishop Edward G. Andrews, who also spoke at the funeral service.

This life of mortal breath is but a suburb of the life Elysium, whose portal we call death. According to the law of affinity, goodness is drawn to goodness. God is good. Bishop Scott was good, he loved goodness; hence by the law of affinity he is now with the good. I would be satisfied to be in such company and with such a Savior. "I am the resurrection and the life; he that believeth in me, though he were dead, yet shall he live; and whoever liveth and believeth in me shall never die" [John 11:25-26]. We know that the latter part of this passage is true, and of course we know, too, that the first part is also true. Bishop Scott, although 60 years ago was dead, believed in Jesus and was made alive in Christ, and having lived a life of faith, he still lives. "There is no death."

Dr. A. J. Kynett spoke briefly, but not less eloquently, upon the dead bishop's solicitude for preachers in making new appointments, at conference, and cited incidents where his sympathy and encouragement had been given and served to cheer up both the young and old. Revs. A. Atwood and G. A. Phoebus also made fitting addresses.

A memorial window in memory of Bishop Scott, in the
old St. Paul's building, in Odessa, Delaware.

The lid was then removed from the casket, and the
hundreds who had assembled at Union Church, to witness the
ceremonies, filed around the casket and took a parting look at
their bishop, minister, neighbor and friend.

The lid was then replaced and loving hands bore the
remains to their last resting place. While the remains were being
taken to the tomb, Mrs. Hutchins sang a beautiful hymn, "I
Would Not Live Alway."

Rev. William Swindells then read from the burial service,
commenting, "Man that is born of woman hath but a short time
to live and is full of misery." He was followed by the Rev. George
W. Miller, who consigned the body to the earth, and by Rev.
Andrew Manship, who read, "And I heard a voice from heaven
saying unto me, Write, Blessed are the dead which die in the
Lord from henceforth: Yea, saith the Spirit, that they may rest
from their labours; and their works do follow them" [Rev. 14: 13].
Rev. T. E. Martindale then recited the Lord's Prayer, in concert
with the other ministers in attendance. Bishop Simpson concluded the services by pronouncing the benediction.

Bishop Scott's grave is directly beside that of his wife, on the opposite side of the monumental shaft of marble in the family burial lot. It is directly in front of the church, and borders on the walk from the gateway to the church door. The tomb is heavily walled with bricks and cement, and arched overtop with bricks tightly cemented.

Beside the minsters mentioned in yesterday's dispatch, the following were in attendance: Revs. R. H. Adams, E. C. Adkins, W. S. E Avery, N. M. Browne, Julius Dodd, J. P. Otis, Charles A. Hill, Dr. George A. Phoebus, A. T. Scott, William W. Warner and John Wilson. J. P. Otis, pastor of Odessa Methodist Episcopal Church, had direction of the ceremonies and conducted them admirably.

Memorial Services in the ME Church on the Death of Bishop Scott

New Castle, July 17 – The services at the Methodist Episcopal Church in this place yesterday were of an impressive character, having special reference to the death of the late Bishop Scott. The church was heavily draped in mourning. Stretching from either end of the platform to the Bible stand was a ground work with this beautiful Scriptural text: "Know ye not that there is a great man fallen this day in Israel" [2 Samuel 3:38]. In the pulpit, upon a table surmounted by a heavy base, was placed a beautiful cross of immortelles embedded in which was the name of Bishop Scott.

After a sermon by the pastor, Rev. N. M. Browne, founded upon 2 Samuel 3:38, he read a sketch of the life of the late bishop, with some data as to the wonderful growth of the church, since the bishop began his ministry in the Philadelphia Conference.

The church will be draped in mourning for a month.

A map showing the territory covered by the Delaware
Conference, which functioned as a conference for black
preachers and churches from 1864 to 1965.

Appendix B
Delaware Conference
Tribute to Bishop Scott

The following resolution was adopted at the 1882 session of the Delaware Conference, which convened in Centerville, Maryland on July 20, just one week after Scott's death. It is preserved in in a bound volume of handwritten minutes of the Delaware Conference, covering the years 1877-1882, in the possession of Zoar United Methodist Church, Philadelphia.

Rev. Bishop Levi Scott, DD, Senior Bishop of the Methodist Episcopal Church, died at his residence near Odessa, Delaware, July 13, 1882, after a protracted career of usefulness in the Church in which he served.

He has filled all of the distinguished places in the Church from the pastorate to the episcopacy.

From the beginning to the end, he manifested himself a friend of the colored race, especially those who were members of the Methodist Episcopal Church.

Twenty-five or thirty years ago, when the freedom of speech was denied, or not allowed to the white preachers in the middle and the more southern States of the Union, and much less, association with the colored people, Bishop Scott (after repeated petitions by some of the leading colored brethren of the North) repulsed the vigorous objections offered by some of the leading men of the Church, and organized what was then known as the Local Conference in the more Northern States, including a part of the state of Delaware.

This was the conception of a thing at that dark period that has proved to be, in this brighter age, a regular organized conference in the Methodist Episcopal Church. We refer to the Delaware Conference; and yet the eighteen or twenty other conferences, a part of which are all, and part a majority, colored members, may be considered the fruit of the magnificent creature rocked in a cradle, in the form of a local conference twenty five or thirty years ago. Bishop Scott was then shaping a destiny for us that has proved more glorious than the eye of the Church or world had thought to look upon for the next half century or more.

His persistent energies and noble philanthropy were not easily satisfied. In 1852 he was elected to the episcopacy, and 1853 he visited the mission work in Liberia, and held the first regular Conference of our Church in that country.

Bishop Scott will not be forgotten when the names of John Brown, Abraham Lincoln, Gen. Ulysses S. Grant, and Gen. James A. Garfield are being read and thought of as the heroes of true national freedom in this country.

Bishop Scott was the originator of the Centenary Biblical Institute in Baltimore, of which Professor Rounds has the honor to be president. He has presided four times over this body, and has visited he conference several times, and always expressed it a gratification to him to do so.

Now this great man has passed away, his work is done; the heaven of eternal repose is gained, and in his footsteps may we tread, until our life's labor is ended, and we the harbor gain, and there greet the beloved father of this, and many other Conferences in the Methodist Episcopal Church.

> W. J. Parker
> N. Young
> H. Jolly
>   Committee

Appendix C
Two Early Sermon Outlines

The following sermons of Scott's are from a handwritten book in the archive at Barratt's Chapel, Federica Delaware. The title on the cover is "Plans of Sermons, 1834." That title, along with short phrases that appear to be memory prompts for stories, indicate that what follows are outlines or briefs, not transcripts of actual preached messages, which would have been much longer, and incorporated a variety of illustrations.

The Infallible Direction

Believe on the Lord Jesus Christ and thou shalt be saved. Acts 16:31

This is the answer of Paul and Silas to the Philippian jailer, who, awakened by the miraculous events which had taken place, inquired what he should do to be saved. And as Paul and Silas (at least the former) were inspired men, this answer must be regarded as furnishing an infallible direction, not only to the jailer, but also to all awakened, penitent sinners. It is, in truth, God's own direction to such, and can never fail, if strictly followed, to lead them to the desired result – to lead them to salvation.

The question which naturally arises when reading or hearing that direction is, "What is its precise import? What does it mean?" I shall first endeavor to answer this question and then urge instant compliance with the exhortation.

I am first to explain the direction given in the text, "Believe on the Lord Jesus Christ."

Before I proceed, however, to do this, it may be proper to direct attention to the specific character of the direction. It differs from other directions recorded in the New Testament. Our Savior, for example, says, "Come unto me, etc." St. Peter says, "Repent and be baptized, etc." "Repent and be converted, etc." Now, it is worthy of remark that faith is not mentioned in any one of these, and that "repentance and self-denial, etc." is not mentioned in the text. How is this? Are not all these suitable directions to seekers? They are, and for the reason that they all amount in the end to the same thing. Faith being supported in these in which it is not mentioned, and repentance, etc. being supported in the text.

The difference is that, in the text, attention is directed to the main points to that which is immediately necessary to salvation. Repentance etc. are necessary to salvation, but not in the same sense that faith is. Between repentance etc. and salvation, faith must intervene; but between faith and salvation nothing intervenes, but salvation follows instantly. So that the meaning of the text is, "Believe etc., and thou shalt be instantly saved." The specific character of the text therefore is that it directs the inquirer to the main thing – to that upon which salvation immediately depends.

Having now adverted to the specific character of the direction, let us give attention to its import.

I do not feel that I am here called upon to attempt any definition of faith, as I do not consider that such definition is necessary to a proper exposition of the text. Indeed, I regard all such attempts as tending to involve the whole subject in confusion, as they divert the attention from the object on which it ought to be fixed. It is a remarkable fact, and full of instruction, that neither our Lord nor any of his disciples gives us any definition of faith, but proceed invariably upon the supposition that the people understand it. St. Paul, even in the case of the heathen jailer, proceeds upon this supposition. Paul says, indeed, [in] Hebrews 11:1 that "faith is the substance, etc." But that is not a definition of faith. He does not state what faith is in itself, but what it is to its possessor – not its nature, but its

A camp meeting, with the preacher's stand in the center.

effect. Now, as our Lord and his apostles assume that the people understand what faith is, may we not assume the same thing? I think we may, and so I think I am relieved from the necessity of any attempt of this kind on the present occasion.

One thing, however, I must do, because it has an important bearing upon the elucidation of the text. I must remind you that faith is a different thing according as it stands related to simple statements of matters of fact, or to persons or promise. As related to simple historical statements, it denotes simple belief that they are true. But as related to persons or promises, it denotes trust also – confidence that the persons are able and willing to do what they assume to do – that the promises will be strictly fulfilled. Accordingly, to believe on the Lord Jesus Christ is to trust in him – to confide that he will accomplish in and for us all he has engaged to do. True, it supposes belief in his history – the record God has given of him – but it implies trust also.

Now, as to "believe on the Lord Jesus Christ" is to trust in him, all that remains to do is to remark the attributes of this trust. It is not then a nominal, but a real heartfelt trust – not a future, but a present trust; not a hesitating and partial, but an unreserved and exclusive trust. The Lord Jesus Christ claims to be the almighty and sole Savior. As the foundation of his claim, he refers us to his person – to his offices – to his redeeming work. And he bids us come unto him – to receive him – to rely upon him; to fly into his arms. The penitent sinner obeys. Letting go of every other trust, he flies to him – he trusts in him – he leans with his entire weight upon him – and so he "believes on him."

Suffer me then to urge you to an immediate compliance with this direction. Believe now on the Lord Jesus Christ. The encouragement held out is that you shall be saved now – "and thou shalt be saved."

But there are obstacles in your way. You say, "I have been a great sinner – I am not sufficiently penitent – am too unworthy – cannot feel; E. Staats' case – must come to the altar; Mr. Wesley's case – have no faith; the little girl.

Our Sanctification the Will of God

This is the will of God, even your sanctification. 1 Thess. 4:3

An object is here presented and a reason stated why we should possess it. The object is sanctification, the reason, the will of God. No object can be more important, no reason, more effective. Let us then direct attention first the object, and then to the reason.

   1.   The object presented is sanctification.

There is not probably in Christian theology a subject on which serious persons are more solicitous and eager for accurate and thorough information than on that here presented. Much has been said and written on it, and yet the question, what is sanctification, is asked and grappled with almost the same intensity as if it had never been answered. No one seems perfectly satisfied; even the best informed seem to suspect some incorrectness or incompleteness in their information and ask for more. It will not then be supposed that I have the vanity to think this question will be set to rest by what I am about to say.

A map showing the territory comprising the Philadelphia Conference from 1844 to 1868. The annual conference, akin to a synod or diocese, is the basic organizational unit of American Methodism. Preachers generally remained members of a single annual conference, as did Levi Scott, until his election as bishop in 1852.

Indeed, it is not my purpose to enter minutely into the subject, to discuss it in all its aspects and bearings. I only intend to present, in as small a compass as practicable, an outline of the Bible doctrine of this subject.

What then is sanctification? In the proper and primary sense, to sanctify is to hallow, to consecrate, to devote to God, to set apart for a sacred use; and sanctification denotes either the act of so consecrating or setting apart, or the state of being so consecrated. In this sense, the word is often used, particularly in the Old Testament, and it is applied not only to rational beings but also to brute creatures and things without life. So we often speak of the sanctification of the Sabbath, and of the dedication or consecration of churches. Now it is obvious that in this sense, sanctification does not imply any change in the nature of the person or thing of which it is predicated, but refers exclusively to its destination or use.

Under the Jewish dispensation, to sanctify often signified to cleanse or purify ceremonially, and to go no farther. An example of this use of the word is furnished by St. Paul. See Hebrews 9:13. Accordingly, sanctification in this sense denotes only an outward, or church purification. But as the term is generally used in the New Testament and in Christian theology, it denotes something moral and spiritual. It denotes that gracious work of God by which the heart is purified from moral defilement or sin; or rather, it denotes that state of the heart, in which, by the Holy Spirit, it is purified from sin. Accordingly, Mr. Watson defines it [as], "that work of God's grace by which we are renewed after the image of God, set apart for his service, and enabled to die to sin and to live unto righteousness."

It will however be better to consider this subject in its relation to the heart or the life. In relation to either, it is the opposite of sin, and it is synonymous with holiness. In the text, it refers to the life. Yet it relates to the life or deportment as the development of the heart. Accordingly, Mr. Watson says, that sanctification is either of *nature*, or of *practice*.

Sanctification supposes on the part of the sinner repentance towards God and faith in our Lord Jesus Christ, and on the part of God, as gracious blessings bestowed by him: pardon, regeneration and adoption. Yet it differs from all of

"The Itinerant," an engraving from the *Ladies Repository*
in 1856, depicting the Methodist circuit-riding preacher.

them. Pardon, regeneration and adoption are concomitants, and
each denotes a gracious act of God, which is instantaneous,
complete at once, and unless the subject fall away, not repeated;
whereas sanctification denotes a permanent state of the heart
and character of the life which yet, if the subject be faithful, is
constantly improving. Justification, regeneration and adoption
are the gate through which a sinner must pass in order to enter
upon the way of holiness; whereas sanctification is holiness itself
– it is "the path of the just that shineth more and more unto the
perfect day" [Proverbs 4:18]. In the former, "fruit of the Spirit" is
produced; in the latter, that fruit is matured and refined. In a
word, sanctification is a pure stream which, taking its rise in
regeneration, flows on and widens as it flows till it empties itself
into the boundless ocean of perfect holiness in heaven. Or is it a
bud, of which having been awakened into life in regeneration,
gradually unfolds itself until, when fully bloomed, it diffuses
around it the fragrance of a sweet smell. Or, in time, it is the

babe in Christ, born in regeneration, and growing up to the fulness of the stature of a perfect man in Christ Jesus.

Such is the object presented in the text – sanctification, holiness of heart and life. Let us now,

2.   Direct attention to the reason why we should possess it: "This is the will of God, even your sanctification" [1 Thessalonians 4:3].

This reason or motive is one of great force and comprehension. It implies that sanctification is both our privilege and duty. It is the will of God – therefore it is our privilege. It is the will of God – therefore it is our duty. And these two considerations ought to be sufficient to urge us to its possession.

i. Sanctification is your privilege. This is the will of God. He permits it – allows it – it is his good pleasure. He has not plan, no decree, no purpose, no disposition against it. There is nothing in his nature or his government in opposition to it. The way then is fully open; there is no impediment. Nay, this is not all. God does not only not oppose, he desires it. It is his will. It is the end of all his dispensations towards us. For this end he spared not his own Son, but gave him up for us all. For this end he gave his word. For this end he sent his Spirit. For this end he instituted his ministry, his ordinances. All are intended to bring us to sanctification, and so to heaven.

By how much sin is a deadly, loathsome evil and sanctification is a desirable good – by just so much ought the fact that the latter is our privilege urge us to its possession. The way is clear – there are no obstructions. Let us then follow hard after it. Nay, God invites and attracts us toward it by all the power of his love and dealings with us. Let us then yield to his sweet influences and sink into his arms.

ii. But secondly, sanctification is your duty. This is the will of God. He enjoins it. But his will is your law. Not to be sanctified is to resist the will of God – to displease him – to incur his wrath. Not to be sanctified is not to be justified – is to fall under condemnation – to fall into hell. By how much then the displeasure of God is to be deprecated, the damnation of hell to be dreaded – even by so much does the fact it is the will of God that we should be sanctified press us to the attainment.

The question of sanctification then, is not a question of mere fitness, or propriety or utility. No, it is one of life or death – of salvation and damnation. Hence, St. Paul says, "without holiness no man shall see the Lord" [Hebrews 12:14]. No man! It matters not who he is, or what are his possessions or attainments. If he lack[s] holiness, that lack is his ruin.

Finally, observe: sanctification is your privilege and duty *now*, your permanent, continuous privilege to duty. Mark the phraseology. This is the will of God. But when? Can he behold sin at any time with allowance?

Do you then, my brethren, enjoy this happy state, possess this character? Are you sanctified? I know your embarrassment in answering affirmatively. You are sensible of so many infirmities, and imperfections, and shortcomings, you can scarcely allow that you are sanctified. You admit indeed that you have been justified etc., but were I sanctified, you say, would I be thus? I answer yes – just thus, and this you will be while you are in the body. Infirmities and imperfections are your burden, and you must groan, being burdened until you are clothed upon with your house which is from heaven. I do not then ask you whether you are sanctified wholly. This you may not be. Yet you should follow hard after it. But are you sanctified? If you are not, mark the phraseology of the text...

A 2018 photograph of historic Scott Methodist Church in Townsend, Delaware, which is no longer active. During Bishop Scott's life and afterward, a number of churches around the country were named in his honor. Several remain active, including the Mount Scott Church in Liberia, and the Scott's United Methodist Church in Trappe, Maryland.

Appendix D
Scott's 1853 Liberia Address

The following message was delivered by Bishop Scott on March 7, 1853 before the Liberia Annual Conference, which Scott convened that day. This was the first time an American bishop of the ME Church presided over an annual conference session outside the continental United States. The message is preserved in the *Journals of the Liberia Annual Conference, ME Church, 1851-1853,* a typed manuscript in the possession of the General Commission on Archives and History in Madison, New Jersey.

Brethren of the Liberia Mission Annual Conference: I esteem it a great Providential privilege to be permitted to salute you personally and in conference assembled. I had heard of you. I had noted your field of labor from year to year. I had read of your toils, privations and success, but I had not the pleasure of a personal acquaintance with any of your number, nor had I any expectations until very recently of ever seeing your faces in the flesh, or of extending personally to you my salutation.

I may say indeed with St. Paul, that I longed to see you, that I might impart to you some spiritual gift to the end that ye might be established, that is (and the explanation is more needed in my case than his) that I might be comforted together with you, by the mutual faith both of you and me [Romans 1:11-12]. And when in the first meeting of the Board of Bishops after my consecration to the responsible office which I now sustain, the question was asked, "who will go to Africa?" I responded in substance, "Here I am, send me." I did not ask indeed to come, for that would have been too much like taking the matter into my own hands. But I signified my readiness for this or any other mission to which it might be the pleasure of the Board to designate me. I had read and heard something of the perils of the ocean, but what has he to do with perils who is striving to move in obedience to the will of God?

I remembered that word, "Lo, I am with you always, even unto the end of the world" [Matthew 28:20]. I thought of the words of the noble Paul: "Neither count I my life dear unto myself that I may finish my course with joy, and the ministry which I have received of the Lord Jesus to testify the gospel of the grace of God" [Acts 20:24]; and was not unmindful of those of the sainted Cox, "Though a thousand fall, let not Africa be given up."[1] The appointment was made and through the good providence of God, I this day stand before you.

I cannot but regard you, my brethren, as occupying a most interesting and important field of labor. You sustain individually, more or less, the double relation of pastors to the flock of Christ, and missionaries to the heathen; and in the latter relation, protected as you are by the civil government, both in the Republic, and in Maryland, in Liberia, you enjoy advantages not possessed by other missionaries in the world. You can live to a great extent within the bounds and in the enjoyment of the blessings of civilization, and yet discharge the important functions of your office to those who sit in darkness and in the shadow of death, while at the same time you are aided in your holy work by the silent but constantly increasing influence of the government which spreads the aegis of its protection over yourselves. Thus situated, if you do not succeed in bringing the heathen into the light of the glorious gospel of Christ, we then abandon the hope of the conversion of the heathen world to Christ, unless God adopts some other method of bringing about this great result than that which seems so already revealed in the gospel. I am aware, my brethren, that you have [seen] long established, and deeply rooted, social and domestic habits of the heathens of this land, together with their almost innumerable superstitions, pose a most stubborn resistance to the gospel.

---

[1] A reference to Rev. Melville B. Cox (1799-1833), pioneer early missionary to Liberia. See page 55.

An 1864 map of Liberia. Bishop Scott's visit in the winter of 1853
helped reinvigorate the Methodist mission conference there.

To this may be added the numerous languages and
dialects spoken by the people, and the difficulty of procuring
competent interpreters though whom to communicate distinctly
and clearly the truths of the gospel. But my brethren, these are
difficulties common to all heathen lands. Besides these, in
almost all other places there is an organized idolatry interwoven
with powerful civil governments watchfully and zealously
guarded and supported by them. This is not the case here. Here
there is no organized religion at all, nor is there, as I can find,
any state establishment watching with more than a panther's eye
all encroachments, real or imaginary, upon its rights; so that,
great as are the difficulties you have to contend with (I
acknowledge they are great), still, the greatest and most fearful
obstacle usually to be encountered within heathen lands does
not exist here at all.

Your situation in this respect is very similar to that of
[Home?] Missionaries' work [among] heathen.[2] Can [it] be
expected to succeed? But you will not fail – you have not wholly
failed – you cannot fail. That word, "Lo, I am with you always,

----

[2]A probable reference to the Home Missionary Society of the
ME Church, which worked domestically in the USA among native peoples.

even to the end of the world" [Matthew 28:20] must ensure your success. And I indulge with pleasure the anticipation that you and your successors, and your brethren of other communions similarly situated with you and their successors, are appointed in the good providence of God to bring the benighted millions of this vast peninsula to the glorious light and liberty of the children of God. True, your progress thus far has been slow – only a few adult natives have been truly converted to the faith and morals of Christianity, and only a few native children have been permanently benefited by the instructions received in the schools. And the consideration of these facts naturally leads one to enquire whether all has been done which might reasonably have been expected. Whether our brethren have been faithfully enterprising, whether they have donated themselves exclusively to their work and labored like men in earnest – like men who feel that a dispensation of the gospel is committed to them, that there is a woe to them if they preach not the gospel; or whether they have to any extent entangled themselves with the affairs of this life by which their ministry has been marred or ruined. But be these things as they may, your progress in the nature of things is likely to be slow; still more may be actually accomplished than it appears on the surface. There may be the laying of the foundation, on which others may build, or you yourself, in the future years.

Thus, one soweth, and another reapeth [John 4:37]. You labor, and others may enter into your labors. The patience of faith, and the labor of love, are specially needed in the field of foreign missions. And it is a cheering thought that in the great Day of final decision, a man is to be graciously regarded according to his works, and not according to the success of his work. I ought not to disguise the fact that I have felt pain in being informed that there is a growing dislike among you to the itinerancy, and it is strongly questioned whether it is adapted to the peculiarities of the work on the Coast, and that individuals of other communions have, when opportunity occurred, contributed to deepen the dissatisfaction by urging the same supposed fact. To others my reply is brief. When they shall show us a plan, not which may be supposed, but which has been proved, to be more efficient in propagating the gospel on this

Coast than an itinerancy, then they will have claims to be heard. But until then, they should be silent and suffer us to manage our own affairs. A tree is known by its fruits.

To our brethren I have but a word now. Is it not probable that the provisions have been overlooked by which the itinerancy is not required on the mission work? The bishop, you are aware, is not allowed to station a preacher in the same place more than two years in succession, except (among others) missionaries in foreign stations. According to this exception, a rigid itinerancy is not required on the field of foreign mission. There a man be stationed one or twenty years in the same place as the necessities of this work may require. Is not this enough? Surely, it can't be desired that a man should be stationed for life in one place, whether to be useful or not, or should anyone desire this? I fear it would be found that he had lost the missionary fire, if indeed, he had not lost the fire of Charity also, and that this is the real difficulty in this case. I have not visited all the stations immediately on the Coast except Marshall, and some of those inland, and I am gratified to learn that the relations of our mission with those of other churches are generally peaceful and harmonious. They ought to be so universally – there is so much need of mutual confidence [and] mutual aid and support among the laborers in the vineyard of our common Master on this Coast, that here especially the spirit of sectarian proselytism ought to be extinct. No enlightened missionary board could ever think of sending one to these shores and of sustaining them here at large expense to proselyte ministers and members of other churches whom they profess to regard as brethren in Christ – certainly ours does not. The noble-spirited Paul [declined] to preach the gospel in certain places lest he should build on another man's foundation [Romans 15:20]. That to the poor, I mean, spirited proselyte, it seems to be glory enough thus to build.

I am happy to say that, in my investigation since I have been on these shores, I have not found a single case in which my brethren have been guilty of the course condemned, and I hope there is not one. Continue, my brethren, to cultivate those friendly relations with brethren of other evangelical churches by observing the obvious principles on which alone such relations

Two photographs of Bishop Levi Scott.

may solidly exist. Respect their claim of church-ship. Respect their disciplinary regulations, particularly in regard to the admission of ministers and members. And never receive either the one or the other unless they bring a certificate of honorable dismissal from the churches from which they brought that certificate, or at least until a fair and honorable understanding [is] lodged with those who have the supervision of him, and all obstacles removed carefully from all the orbs and measures of proselytism, so that others should depart from these principles. Never retaliate by following their examples, but guard yourselves the best way you can from the effects of the measures they may be pleased to adopt. I may have many other things to say, but it will perhaps be more appropriate to say them when the subject comes up to which they relate. I close by reminding you of the wholesome directions of our excellent *Discipline* to preachers while attending Conference.

Appendix E
Bishop Scott's 1876 Address

In 1876, Levi Scott marked the fiftieth anniversary of his admission to the Philadelphia Conference as an itinerant preacher. That spring, he was presiding over the annual session of the Wilmington Conference, which had been formed in 1868, by separating from the Philadelphia Conference its territory in Delaware, Maryland and Virginia. This had been the region where Scott's faith was formed, his calling to ministry received, and his first appointments located. Scott was asked to preach his "semi-centennial" sermon during the Wilmington Conference session, which he did on March 20. The following text is taken from *Wilmington Conference Minutes* (1876), 73-80.

"Say not thou, what is the cause that the former days were better than these? For thou dost not inquire wisely concerning this." (Eccl. 7:1)

The weakness here censured is common to all ages and all people. It affects mainly, it is presumed, persons advanced in years who have failed to keep even pace with the progress of their times and who, being therefore out of harmony with the people and circumstances around them, and unable to appreciate the beneficial changes which have occurred within their own days, look back to "the former days" of their early years as to a kind of golden age in comparison with which the passing days are regarded with dissatisfaction and complaint. This I have called a weakness – perhaps it is not a sin, yet it covers a lack of wisdom and a want of trust in the overruling providence of God, and cannot fail to impair and damage both comfort and usefulness. "Sufficient unto the day is the evil thereof" [Matthew 6:34], applies with equal pertinence and justice to all days, whether former or current, and the truly good man who "redeems the time because the days are evil" [Ephesians 5:16] will find in all days more occasions for gratitude and thankfulness than for murmuring and complaint. "A good man," says Solomon, "shall be satisfied from himself" [Proverbs 14:14] – he has in himself a source of satisfaction which is not materially affected by the times.

Closing in a few days my fiftieth year in the itinerant ministry of the ME Church, and being in the 74th year of my life, I can, without sensitiveness, be placed in the category of aged men, being indeed more aged than any of my living colleagues, or any of my deceased colleagues, except Bishops Whatcoat, McKendree and Morris; yet I felicitate myself with the thought that I am touched but slightly, if at all, with the weakness criticized by the sacred writer. I do not indeed regard change as synonymous with progress, and do, on the contrary, think that some changes are not for the better but for the worse. Yet I recognize, with devout gratitude to Almighty God, the great fact that there has been, in the last fifty years, a real and wonderful progress, not only in general society, and in the Protestant churches generally, but also, and especially in the church of my earliest and latest fellowship, the Methodist Episcopal Church.

This last point I at first thought would make the subject of this discourse and made some preparations accordingly. But I soon found that it was too large in all its dimensions to be treated with any satisfaction in the brief space of one hour. I have therefore adopted a subject less imposing indeed – the Philadelphia Conference of 1826 and its growth and development in the last fifty years.

It may not be out of place to premise that the first conference of Methodist itinerants ever convened in this country was held in Philadelphia, July 14th, 1773. It consisted of ten preachers, representing 1,160 members. The preachers were all of English birth, except William Watters, who was born in Baltimore County, Maryland, October 16th, 1751. He was the first native American itinerant Methodist preacher in America. This

Image of an early Methodist conference.
----

small conference of ten preachers, with 1,160 members, grew in fifty-two years, according to the minutes of 1825, into 15 annual conferences with 1,314 preachers and 341,114 members; and in 102 years, according to last year's minutes, into 81 conferences in this and other lands, besides large and flourishing missions, with 10,923 preachers and 1,580,550 members, after having been depleted by four secessions, the last of which alone carried off about 800 preachers and more than a half a million of members. Looking at these facts, who can help exclaiming, "What hath God wrought!" [Numbers 23:23]. I turn now to my subject.

The Philadelphia Conference of 1826 embraced the states of New Jersey and Delaware, the eastern shores of Maryland and Virginia, and so much of Pennsylvania as is now embraced in the present Philadelphia Conference, together with Harrisburg. This territory was divided into five districts: the Philadelphia, the Chesapeake, the Delaware, the West and the East Jersey Districts, and these were subdivided into 51 pastoral charges, mostly four-weeks' circuits, and on these districts and other charges were stationed 96 preachers, sixteen of whom were supernumeraries, for all supernumeraries in those days were assigned to fields of labor. Indeed, Ezekiel Cooper, then a supernumerary, was appointed to West Jersey district as presiding elder, with, as it would seem, Joseph Osborn, also a supernumerary, as assistant. The statistics of that conference report 103 traveling preachers and 36,655 members, and nothing more. To say that the statistical tables of that day were defective as compared with our present tables is not surprising. There has, of course, been progress in the last fifty years in the clerical work of collecting and arranging the statistics as in other things, and our present full and beautiful tables are the result of a very gradual progress under the direction of many capable minds.

But the statistics of 1826 are defective as compared with the then current facts. They report traveling preachers and members, but are silent about deaths, baptism, local preachers, churches and parsonages, Sunday schools and benevolent collections. And yet, there were deaths in those days, and baptisms, and local preachers, and churches and parsonages, and yes, benevolent collections, at least for conference claimants and for missions. It would be interesting to know the facts in all these particulars. But whence is this knowledge to be derived? We know, indeed, from other sources, that the Missionary Society of the ME Church had been organized seven years before, in 1819 – and that $4,140 were collected for the missionary cause in the whole church in 1825, and we do not doubt that the Philadelphia Conference contributed her full share of that amount. And we know, too, that the Methodists in this country from the very beginning of their work, cherished a lively interest in the religious cultivation of the children, and that the first Sunday school in this country was formed by Mr. Asbury himself in the house of a Mr. Crenshaw, in Virginia, so early as 1786. But the statistics of those days are silent.

One item in the scanty statistics of 1826 is noticeable and suggestive. The members are reported in two columns, one of white and one of colored members. This practice began in 1786 and was discontinued in 1860. It brings to mind an incident, belonging to the same category, which occurred under my own observation, in a session of the Philadelphia Conference, in 1838 in Asbury Church in this city. A young man in the full vigor of youthful life was recommended to be received on trial. It was whispered about in conference that that young

Asbury ME Church, Wilmington, Delaware, where the 1876
session of the Wilmington Conference was held,
and Bishop Scott delivered his anniversary address.

---

man was an abolitionist of a very pronounced type; that he not
only indulged free thought on the vexed question, but free
speech also, and sometimes in public places, and it was felt that
it would not do to admit him into the conference, even on trial,
unless he would give a pledge to, at least, restrain his utterances.
A committee of three was appointed of the best men in the
conference to wait on him and to get from him, if practicable,
this pledge. But the young man was firm, was stubborn it was
thought, and promptly refused to give any pledge, and so he was
not admitted.[1]

Now need I ask, what is the explanation of these strange
procedures, reporting the colored members of the church in a
separate column, and refusing to admit a young man of fair

---

[1]Scott is referencing his friend Rev. Lucius C. Matlack (1816-1883),
who was in the assembly as the bishop spoke. After his rejection by the
Philadelphia Conference, Matlack was admitted into the New England
Conference. He later left the ME Church with Rev. Orange Scott and other
abolitionists to form the Wesleyan Connection. He returned after the Civil
War to the Philadelphia Conference, and became a charter member of the
Wilmington Conference when it was formed in 1868. In 1876, Matlack was
appointed to serve in Middletown, Delaware.

promise on trial in the conference because he was an abolitionist? Those were "slavery times," as the colored people down south would say, times when the system of slavery in this country dominated the minds of even good men, when it could not control their persons and services, and these questionable procedures were deemed only prudent recognitions of its dominance. But a change has occurred, a progress has been achieved, in a way, too, which we knew not. The column of colored members has disappeared from the minutes, and that very man who was denied admission to probation in the conference because he was an abolitionist is now, with unchanged, though quiescent, convictions, an unchallenged and honored member of this conference. The tragic story is soon told. The Slave Power, grown impatient of criticism, not by the federal government, but by individuals in and out of Congress, and by voluntary associations, appealed to the sword to establish slavery forever in this country as the cornerstone of a Christian government and a Christian civilization, and to place it beyond the reach of annoying criticism. But that dreadful power proved to be wayward and would not obey the behests of those who made the appeal, but turning upon its employers, it mercilessly abolished the Slave Power and destroyed slavery forever! January first, 1863 is epochal. Abraham Lincoln is immortal, by the issue on that day, as a war measure, of the Proclamation of Emancipation. We can now sing, as never before

> The star spangled banner,
>   O long may it wave
> O'er the land of the free
>   And the home of the brave.

I was not present, as I have said, at the session of 1826. I met the conference for the first time in Smyrna, in 1827. It held its session in the Friends meeting house, a small, plain building, in the outskirts of the village, the church being reserved for religious services. Assembled in a plain house, they appeared a grave and plain body of men, not rude, but plain – plain in dress, plain in speech, plain in manners. They were the representatives of plain churches and a plain people. Not one of them had ever sat on a cushioned seat, or walked on a carpeted aisle, or stood on a carpeted platform, or kneeled on a cushioned kneeling stool in a Methodist house of public worship. They were clad, almost to a man, in what has been called "the Methodist preacher uniform" of that day. The broad brimmed hats did not, of course, appear as they were in conference session. But their coats were either straight or round breasted or a modification between the two, single breasted, also that would button to the chin. Their neck dress consisted of a plain white cravat, with or without stock, concealing the collar of the shirt, and presenting in front a plain smooth surface, or a single or double bow according to the varying tastes of the parties. The hair betokened nothing in its adjustment, but the most modest and natural plainness, being combed down smoothly over the forehead, and their cleanly shaven faces exhibited neither mustache, goatee, nor any other fanciful arrangement now so popular even among ministers. As to the hair, indeed, there were some notable exceptions. Solomon Sharp, a most venerable but eccentric man, wore his parted in the middle and hanging in heavy ringlets upon his broad and massive shoulders. Lawrence McCombs wore his combed smoothly back, revealing a noble forehead, while Lawrence Lawrenson, a gifted man but uncomfortably low in self appreciation, presented a bold and martial aspect, his rather short, steel-mixed hair standing plumb upright on his head.

Young as I was, and inexperienced in conference business, I soon detected the leader of this body – the man with the wen – a large wen pendent from the right jaw and resting in the wide fold of an enormous white cravat, a deformity it would have been in another, but in him, distinctive, and even comely. It was Ezekiel Cooper, now sixty-four years of age. The words of Job might be fitly applied to him, only changing the first person to the third. "Unto him men gave ear, and waited and kept silence at his counsel" [Job 29:21]. He was the masterly unraveler of tangled and confused discussion, a preacher of great and almost resistless power.

There were, however, other representative men in that body only less distinguished. I may name Lawrence McCombs, Thomas Morrell, Thomas Ware, Henry Boehm – the centenarian

Left: Rev. Solomon Sharp (1771-1836), a fiery evangelistic preacher, popular in the Delaware Valley region. Right: Rev. Ezekiel Cooper (1763-1847), trusted lieutenant of Bishop Asbury, and second leader of the Methodist publishing house.

----

so lately gone to heaven – Solomon Sharp, Henry White, David Daily, Joseph Lybrand, Lawrence Lawrenson and Charles Pitman, just rising to prominence. Such was the Philadelphia Conference of 1826.

The growth and development of this body in the last fifty years may be presented in a nutshell. The conference of 1826 was divided into five districts and 51 charges, mostly four-weeks' circuits; reporting 103 traveling preachers and 36,655 members. Now that conference has developed into five conferences, and a small fraction of a sixth, divided into 24 districts and 764 pastoral charges, mostly stations, and reporting in last year's minutes 770 traveling preachers and 153,402 members and probationers. The minutes of 1826 reported no local preachers, no baptisms, no churches and no parsonages, no Sunday school scholars and no benevolent collections; though the parsonages were then probably all rented, and both they and the churches were such that we would judge to be very inferior in style and finish and comfort; and the Sunday schools were few and small, and confined probably to the large cities; and the collections, both for the conference claimants and the missionary cause were very inconsiderable. Now the minutes of the five conferences report 903 local preachers, 1,301 churches, as, probably, worth $9,631,736; 356 parsonages, probably worth $1,331,660; 14,862 baptisms; 148,630 Sunday school scholars; $26,231.80 for conference claimants; $92,401.10 for the missionary cause. Moreover, the minutes now report for causes which have come up in the progress of the church since 1825: $2,802.25 for the Sunday School Union; $3,585.59 for the Tract Society; $10,591.37 for the Church Extension Society; $4,235.25 for the Women's Foreign Missionary Society; $4,984.89 for Freedman's Aid Society; and $3,570 for the Education Board. These facts and figures show a most encouraging growth and outspread of that old Mother Conference of 1826.

Suppose now we take up some special line of illustration selected from this general exhibit – we shall find the result ever the same. Whether we take the general improvement of the ministry, or the membership, or the Sunday schools, or the churches, or the parsonages, the watchword emblazoned everywhere is, Onward! Let us take the instance of church edifices. In 1826 we had, in this city, two small, unsightly and but moderately comfortable churches, known as the Old Asbury, and the Old Ezion. Now we have six large and beautiful church edifices in good style and finish, one costly and elegant, and all with suitable accommodations for prayer and class meetings and for Sunday schools, besides two or three neat and comfortable mission chapels. In Philadelphia, we had nine churches, arranged in three pastoral charges, all of inferior quality, the best being, perhaps, St. George's, before its later improvements. Now we have in that city some 68 church edifices, all of them more or less in the modern style of church architecture, and some of them large and elegant, and all of them provided more or less perfectly with modern accommodations for church work. In Camden, New Jersey, we had in 1826 one small church, very inferior in every respect. Now we have in that city eight churches, generally large, commodious and beautiful. In Trenton, we had one small, very plain church. Now we have eight, all of modern build, and some of them large and elegant. In Newark, New Jersey, we then had one small church in better

Left: Rev. Thomas Ware (1758-1842), who had been present at the
1784 Christmas Conference which established the Methodist
Episcopal Church. Right: Rev. Henry Boehm (1775-1875), who
traveled with Bishop Francis Asbury. Both men, known to the
young Levi Scott in the Philadelphia Conference, were links
to the earliest days of American Methodism (*St. George's*).

----

finish, indeed, than was usual in that day. Now we have ten,
many of them large and elegant.

But let us turn our eyes southward: New Castle, Odessa
(then called Cantwell's Bridge), Middletown, Smyrna, Frederica,
Milford, Seaford, Laurel, Salisbury, Fairmount, Cambridge,
Easton, St. Michael's, Centreville, Chestertown, Still Pond,
Elkton, Newport and Newark. All then belonged to four weeks'
circuits, with small, unsightly churches. Now they are all
stations having their own pastors, and have neat, commodious,
and handsome church edifices. Indeed, the whole face of
Methodism, within the territory of that old conference, is dotted
over and beautified, even in rural districts, with neat and
comfortable houses of public worship, many of them with spires
pointing up toward to the Pilgrims' Home. But above all, we
must not omit to note, with adoring gratitude, that we have in
our churches a blessed and efficient evangelism. Our pastors and

teachers have not forgotten that they are evangelists also, disciplining men as well as baptizing and teaching them. And God has graciously given us powerful and wide-spreading revivals of primitive Christianity in very many of our churches, and the evangelism of the churches, combining with the evangelism of Moody and Sankey, and others, is spreading the holy fire all around. And let it spread.

Let me now add that the growth and progress of the Philadelphia Conference of 1826 is a fair type of the growth and progress of the whole ME Church in the last 50 years. Confined in 1826 to a narrow strip along the Atlantic coast, she has followed the lines of settlements east, north, west and south, until now, her conferences, districts, and pastoral charges are spread out over all the states and most of the territories of the Union. They span the vast swell of the Rocky Mountains and deploy over the broad slopes of the Pacific coast. Nor has she stopped there, but has gone abroad to distant and heathen lands, and has conferences in Mexico, South America, China, Japan, Scandinavia, Bulgaria, and even in Italy, under the shadow of the Vatican.

I will now close with dwelling for a few minutes on two solemn and suggestive facts which have been brought to mind in the progress of this discourse. One is, the members of the conference of 1826 have all been gathered to their fathers except for seven. These survivors are Bartholomew Weed, Matthew Sorin, Anthony Atwood, James H. Dandy, Thomas B. Sergeant, Pharaoh A. Ogden and myself.

Bartholomew Weed is 83 years of age, has been 59 years in the itinerant ministry, resides in Newark, New Jersey, and sustains a supernumerary relation to the Newark Conference. But practically [he] is effective, preaching once every Sabbath afternoon to the prisoners in Essex County Prison, and often also, morning or evening, in some one of the city churches. He is in good health and spirits, writes with a steady mind and steady hand, is happy in his domestic relations, and is enjoying the sweet, mellowed scenes of life's setting sun, peacefully awaiting the call of the Master.

Matthew Sorin is in his 75th year, has been 53 years in the itinerant field, resides in South Chester, and is doing earnest

Detail of one of the marble slabs on the wall of St.
George's Church, Philadelphia, which list all the
appointed preachers since 1769. Levi Scott served
there, 1828-1830, and his name appears along with
several of the colleagues whom he recalls in his speech.

----

and efficient service in South Chester charge. His health is good,
and his natural force is but slightly, if at all, abated. He is calmly
looking for the mercy of our Lord Jesus Christ unto eternal life,
hoping to finish his labor and his life in the conference of his
early fellowship, and in the presence of his brethren.

Anthony Atwood is in the 75th year of his life, and the
51st of his itinerant ministry. He resides in Philadelphia, is in
good health and vigor of body and of mind, and though nomi-
nally a supernumerary, is really effective, doing perhaps as much
work for God in the church as any pastor in that great city. He is

comfortably provided for, and in happy association with the wife of his youth, he is peacefully enjoying the serene evening of a lengthened and well-spent life.

James H. Dandy was born in Ireland in 1798, and united with the Philadelphia Conference in 1825, He resides in Rahway, has been superannuated several years, greatly broken by inflammatory rheumatism, but is now in better health and able to get about a little in good weather. He is comfortable in his circumstances, happy in his domestic relations, and living in joyous hope of eternal life. He lost his youngest son while storming Fort Gregg, before Petersburg, the day before the fall of Richmond. Another son is a graduate of West Point, a major and quartermaster in the regular army, stationed at Buffalo, [and] is wealthy and happy in his family.

Thomas B. Sergeant was born March 30th, 1805, admitted on trial in the Philadelphia Conference in 1825. He has been since 1866 an honored member of the ME Church, South, lives in Baltimore, was superannuated in 1872, and has since ranged abroad over the southern states and the Pacific coast, doing what he could. He is now prostrated with, as he says, "acute chronic disease," writes little and with difficulty, though formerly a ready and beautiful scribe, and [who] served the General Conference of our church in three sessions, 1836, 1840 and 1844, as secretary. He writes that "his flesh and heart are failing," and asks prayer "that God may be the strength of his heart and his portion forever" [Psalm 73:26].

Pharaoh A. Ogden was born July 28th, 1799 and joined the Philadelphia Conference in 1828. He is a supernumerary in the Cincinnati Conference, and resides at Sidney, Ohio. He says "I am what the people call a well-preserved old man. My health has been remarkably good. My natural force is not much abated. My eye is not yet dim. I have never used spectacles and now read the finest print with as much ease as when but about twenty years of age. I can preach twice a day without more than ordinary fatigue. Pulpit labors are to me both a pleasure and a profit, and my desire is to cease, at once, to work and live."

As to the seventh member of this small remnant of the conference of 1826, I need say little. He is before you and you know him. His health, never vigorous since 1829, is now, perhaps, quite as good as it has been for many years, and his thirstings for God, for the living God, were never stronger than they are now. How striking and appropriate in this whole connection are the words of the poet:

> Like leaves on trees
> The race of men is found,
> Now green in youth,
> Now withering on the ground;
> So generations in their turn decay,
> So flourish these when those have passed away.

The generation of Methodist preachers of 1826 is now nearly all passed away, and the few who remain give unmistakable attestations of the great fact so beautifully formulated by Isaiah, "We all do fade as a leaf" [Isaiah 64:6].

The other fact to which I alluded is still more touching, especially to me. Of my own class of 1826, only two remain, J. H. Dandy and myself. George G. Cookman, Joseph Iliff, Robert Gerry and Thomas J. Thompson are gone to their heavenly homes. Joseph Iliff was the eldest member of the class and finished his work first. He was born in Bucks County, Pennsylvania, December 15th, 1789, and died in Centreville, Maryland, August 8th, 1830. He was a good man and an acceptable and useful preacher.

George G. Cookman was born in England, October 21st, 1800, and came to this country in 1825. His career as an itinerant minister was short and brilliant. In 1839 and 1840 he was chaplain to the US Senate. March 11th, 1841, he took passage on board the ill-fated steamer *President*, for England, intending to return in a few months. This is the last entry in the known history of his life. A profound silence, unbroken by a single utterance, broods over the dreadful catastrophe in which he perished with all his fellow voyagers. "He was not, for God took him" [Genesis 5:24].

Robert Gerry was born January 30th, 1799, and died in this city May 9th, 1856 in the fifty-seventh year of his age. His record is honorable. His last charge was Asbury in this city. He sleeps in Jesus.

Thomas Jefferson Thompson was born March 13th, 1803, and died November 29th, 1874, in the seventy-second year of his life, and the forty-ninth year of his itinerant ministry. In 1828 he and I were thrown together as junior preachers at St. George's charge in Philadelphia, and in the course of that year a friendship grew up between us which death has not severed, for death has no power over Christian friendship. He was a good man, an able, though not a popular preacher, a wise counselor, an admirable administrator of church law. His record is honorable throughout. He was the living embodiment of the twelve rules of a Methodist preacher: diligent, but never fussy; serious, never sour; avoiding lightness, jesting and foolish talking; prudent in his intercourse with all; free from suspicion and evil speaking; tender of the reputation of others; kind and faithful to those under his care; ashamed only of sin and meanness; punctual; a man of one work; and a true son in the gospel; asking nothing, declining nothing; and doing in good faith the work assigned to him. He passed to his rest through a strait gate of unutterable sufferings. Peace to his memory!

And now, our classmates gone, Brother Dandy and I have advanced to the front, and stand side by side on the bald, bleak bluff of the cold river. Yet thanks be to God who gives us the victory though our Lord Jesus Christ! We do not dread its chilling waves, up-borne and enraptured with the prospect beyond "the land of Beulah and the Delectible Mountains."[2]

May the admonition of our Lord, "Be ye also ready, for in such an hour as ye think not, the Son of Man cometh" [Matthew 24:44], be ever sounding in our ears until our work is done and we are safe at home.

---

[2]A reference to Bunyan's *Pilgrim's Progress*, and the view of the celestial city which the Pilgrims could see from the "Delectible Mountains."

A photograph of Bishop Scott from a *carte de visite,*
c. 1860s *(Lovely Lane Museum).*

Appendix F:
Bishop Scott and Eugenics

In its 2008 General Conference, the United Methodist Church adopted a statement entitled, "Repentance for Support of Eugenics," expressing regret and apologizing for past support by Methodist leaders. During the early twentieth century, the eugenics movement promoted sterilization and restricted immigration for "inferior" peoples in the US and elsewhere, and was a significant influence behind Nazi policies of genocide. The 2008 resolution includes the statement, "Methodist bishops endorsed one of the first books circulated to the US churches promoting eugenics." The footnote to that sentence references a book published in 1871 by George Henry Napheys, entitled *The Transmission of Life* (Philadelphia: J. Fergus), with the note, "endorsed by Bishop Levi Scott and Bishop T. A. Morris, both of the Methodist Episcopal Church." (In the 2008 resolution, the author's name is incorrectly spelled as "Naply.")

Scott's endorsement was a single sentence, referring to a testimonial by Rev. John Todd, a prominent Congregationalist minister and founder of Mount Holyoke Seminary, and reads as follows: "I partake largely of the favorable opinion of Dr. Todd, and wish your work great success." Other endorsements, found in a section at the back of the volume, include those of Rev. Horace Bushnell, an Episcopal bishop named Clark, and the presidents of a number of colleges and universities, including Amherst, Indiana State and Cornell. The book was also endorsed by several prominent physicians and periodicals.

George H. Napheys
(1842-1876), author
of an 1871 book endorsed
by Bishop Scott.

Napheys may be considered something of a "proto-eugenicist," an early importer to the United States of concepts just beginning to circulate in Europe. Napheys combined ideas from Charles Darwin, the Bible, Aristotle and practices of animal husbandry (among others), to present what was described by the publisher as a "strictly scientific" analysis of issues surrounding marriage, procreation and physical health.

Much of the book (a copy of which was obtained by the author) is about the biology of sex and disease, a nineteenth-century version of modern day sex education classes. More troublesome to modern minds (given subsequent history) is Napheys' advice to young men in their choice of wives, that they select only those of superior health, heredity and moral character, in order to produce healthier and more socially productive children, thus uplifting society and positively influencing the evolution of the human race.[1]

At this early date of 1871, however, full-blown eugenics had not yet developed; nor, for a dozen more years, would the

---

[1] A summary and analysis of Napheys' book may be found in Amy Laura Hall, *Conceiving Parenthood: American Protestantism and the Spirit of Reproduction* (Grand Rapids: Eerdmans, 2008), 221-230.

term "eugenics" even be coined. The more repugnant features of early twentieth century eugenics were not yet in evidence, and many early supporters of the ideas articulated by Naphys and others regarded them as being about improving the physical strength, health and other positive qualities of the next generation.

While Napheys' ideas undoubtedly helped to lay an intellectual foundation for the fully formed theories of later eugenicists, it is dubious to suggest that Bishop Scott would have endorsed subsequent abuses, especially given his activities in support of the uplift and empowerment of Africans and African Americans, and all based on a one-sentence testimonial. To link Levi Scott's name to all the connotations with which the term "eugenics" are associated in the twenty-first century is historically anachronistic and unfair to the man.

Notes

Introduction

1. Charles D. Lore, *Address of Chief Justice Lore at the Methodist Episcopal Church, November 18, 1901* (1901), 18.

Chapter 1: Anne Scott's Boy

1. Sources on Scott's family include James Mitchell, *The Life and Times of Levi Scott, DD* (New York: Phillips & Hunt, 1885), 12-15, 24-25; H. Clay Reed., ed., *Delaware, A History of the First State: Personal and Family Records*, Vol III (New York: Lewis Historical Publishing Company, 1947), 58; and *Biographical and Genealogical History of the State of Delaware* (Chambersburg: J. M. Runk & Co., 1899), 1232.

2. Mitchell, 14, 26. Church records show Thomas Scott (1772-1803) received on trial in 1803 and assigned to the Queen Anne (Maryland) Circuit, as the assistant to Rev. James Moore. No memoir of Thomas Scott was published after his death in the conference minutes.

3. *Philadelphia Methodist*, July 20, 1882; *Wilmington Conference Minutes* (1882), 45; Mitchell, 32; and "Bishop Levi Scott," in *Journal of the General Conference* (New York: Phillips & Hunt, 1884), 510. On early Methodist rejection of violins, see Adam Wallace, *The Parson of the Islands* (Philadelphia, 1861), 187-189; and William H. Williams, *The Garden of Amer-*

ican Methodism, The Delmarva Peninsula, 1769-1820 (Wilmington: The Peninsula Conference, 1984), 156-157.

4. Quoted in Mitchell, 26.

5. Williams, *Garden of American Methodism*, 39, 73, 87. The Methodist Episcopal Church is the predecessor denomination to today's United Methodist Church.

6. *Philadelphia Methodist*, July 20, 1882; and *Wilmington Conference Minutes* (1882), 45.

7. Mitchell, 31.

8. Mitchell, 32-33; *Philadelphia Methodist*, July 20, 1882.

9. Mitchell, 16, relates that Levi's first apprenticeship in 1819 was in "Georgetown DC," but it is possible the location was Georgetown, Delaware, a town about 60 miles south of Odessa in Sussex County; or Georgetown, Maryland, located less than 40 miles to the southwest, where Levi's mother is believed to have had relatives. As an immigrant from Ireland, Mitchell probably did not know Delaware well, and had worked in the nation's capital during the civil war. It is possible that he saw Georgetown and assumed it to be the one he knew in the District of Columbia. The same reference to "Georgetown, DC" is found on page 28 as part of the transcript of Scott's autobiographical sketch, with the additional detail that the apprenticeship was with a relative named W. Feust. But without the original manuscript in the bishop's own hand, we cannot be sure if the "DC" was in Scott's narrative, or added by Mitchell as editor.

10. "A Brief History of Old Union" in *58th Anniversary "Old Union" Church Society* (Booklet: October 12, 1997); and Frank R. Zebley, *The Churches of Delaware* (Wilmington, 1947), 190.

11. Mitchell, 31-32.

12. Mitchell, 34.

13. Mitchell, 18, 35-37; and William H. Williams, *Slavery and Freedom in Delaware, 1639-1865* (Wilmington: Scholarly Resources, 1996), 226. Lee Chapel, predecessor of today's Lee-Haven United Methodist Church of Townsend, was incorporated in September 1824. *Inventory of the Church Archives of Delaware* (Works Progress Administration, 1940), Binder #1; Delaware State Archives.

14. Mitchell, 36-38.

15. John A. Roche, "Bishop Levi Scott," *Methodist Review* 68:2 (July 1882), 509.

16. Mitchell, 43-44. The meetings in Odessa apparently ended at some point. Today's St. Paul's United Methodist Church dates its origin to an 1830 revival which converted several young men, including Levi's brother, Thomas. A burned home was rebuilt into a first building, known as "Old Bat Church," and dedicated in 1833. This was replaced by a substantial brick church, dedicated in October 1852 by Bishop Levi Scott. *Memorials of the Semi-Centennial of St. Paul's ME Church, Odessa, Delaware, 1833-1883* (Wilmington: The Conference Worker, 1883); and Zebley, 188. In the late

1950s, the congregation moved to a new home on Main Street. The old High Street church has been preserved by the Women's Club of Odessa.

17. Mitchell, 29-31, 43.

18. Arnold Naudain was also a leading member of Union Church; his name heads of the list of signers endorsing Scott as a candidate for ministry, in his recommendation of January 30, 1825. Mitchell, 54; and Naudain House, National Register of Historic Places Inventory–Nomination Form, available at https://npgallery.nps.gov /NRHP/GetAsset/ 821a8b62-dbbb-4f0b-8aa8-8add930f66cd.

19. *Philadelphia Methodist*, July 20, 1882.

Chapter 2: Circuit Riding Preacher

1. Quoted in Lester Ruth, *A Little Heaven Below: Worship at Early Methodist Quarterly Meetings* (Nashville: Kingswood Books, 2000), 183, from an 1857 recollection of Rev. David Lewis.

2. Levi Scott, "Semi-Centennial Sermon," in *Wilmington Conference Minutes* (1876), 74.

3 "Bishop Levi Scott," in *Journal of the General Conference*, op. cit., 511; Roche, "Bishop Levi Scott," 504.

4. Levi Scott to John Lattomus, January 31, 1827, F. D. Leete Collection on Methodist Bishops, Bridwell, Southern Methodist University.

5. Mitchell, 57-58.

6. Nathan O. Hatch, *The Democratization of American Christianity* (New Haven; Yale University Press, 1989), 87.

7. Rev. James Reed (1760-1843) joined the Philadelphia Conference in 1808, and in 1830 transferred to the Ohio Conference. *Minutes of the Annual Conferences of the Methodist Episcopal Church, for the Years 1839-1845*, Vol. III (New York: T. Mason and G. Lane, 1840), 585.

8. John Lednum, *A History of the Rise of Methodism in America* (Philadelphia: By the Author, 1859), 262. James Bateman (1775-1830) joined the Philadelphia Conference in 1806. While in Wilmington, Delaware in 1812-1813, a dispute between him and the leadership of the first all-black congregation on the Peninsula, Ezion Church, prompted a split which created the African Union Methodist Protestant (AUMP) Church, led by Peter Spencer. Williams, *Garden of American Methodism*, 116; and *Minutes of the Annual Conferences of the Methodist Episcopal Church, for the Years 1773-1828*, Vol. I (New York: T. Mason and G. Lane, 1840), 118-119.

9. Anthony Atwood, "Early Methodism in Philadelphia," *Philadelphia Methodist*, April 8, 1880.

10. Samuel Doughty (1794-1828), a Philadelphia native, had only joined the Philadelphia Conference in 1823; his sermons were described as "frequently truly eloquent." *Minutes of the Annual Conferences of the Methodist Episcopal Church, for the Years 1829 to 1839*, Vol. II (New York: Mason and Lane, 1840), 38. Rev. Jacob Gruber (1778-1850) joined the

Philadelphia Conference in 1800, and was serving as a presiding elder in the Baltimore Conference at the time of his controversial sermon and arrest. See Brand W. Eaton, "Jacob Gruber's 1818 Campmeeting Sermon" in *Methodist History* 37:4 (July 1999), 242-252; and W. P. Strickland, *Life of Jacob Gruber* (New York: Carlton & Porter, 1860).

11. Rev. Manning Force (1789-1862) joined the Philadelphia Conference in 1811, and his long ministry included six appointments as a presiding elder, and six times serving as a delegate to General Conference. *Newark Conference Minutes* (1862), 38-39.

12. Anthony Atwood, "Recollections of City Methodism," *Philadelphia Methodist*, May 13, 1880.

13. *Wilmington Conference Minutes* (1880), 47-48.

14. John A. Roche, *Autobiography and Sermons* (New York: Eaton and Mains, [1898]), 57-58, 86.

15. Mitchell, 252-253. This quote is recorded somewhat differently in the version that appears in the *Philadelphia Methodist* of July 27, 1882, and in the transcription of the funeral printed in Appendix A, page 103.

16. Roche, "Bishop Levi Scott," 502. Roche also describes a sermon of Scott's in Smyrna, Delaware on Acts 19:2, remarking, "Fifty-three years have not effaced the memory of that triumphant night."

17. The historian of Philadelphia's Ebenezer ME Church recalled that Scott "emphasized in his preaching the doctrine of sanctification." Scott served there as part of St. George's Circuit in 1829, and again, as a stand-alone appointment in 1837. *History of Ebenezer Methodist Episcopal Church of Southwark, Philadelphia* (Philadelphia: J. B. Lippincott Company, 1890), 87, 106-107.

18. Mitchell, 151.

19. Roche, "Bishop Levi Scott," 497.

20. Levi Scott to George C. M. Roberts, January 25, 1856; Lovely Lane Museum and Library, Baltimore.

21. *Philadelphia Methodist*, July 27, 1882.

22. Levi Scott, "Semi-Centennial Sermon," 80.

23. Levi Scott to John Lattomus, January 31, 1827, F. D. Leete Collection.

24. Roche, "Bishop Levi Scott," 508.

25. William McDonald and John Searles, *The Life of Rev. John S. Inskip* (Boston: McDonald and Gill, 1885), 17-18.

Chapter 3: Rising Star

1. Statistics are from the Philadelphia Conference *Minutes* of 1834 and 1836; on the significance of quarterly conferences, see Lester Ruth, *A Little Heaven Below*, op. cit. After 1912, when bishops were assigned to particular conferences, the role of presiding elder changed, as did its title, to district superintendent.

2. Frank John Urquhart, *A History of the City of Newark, New Jersey*, 2 Vols. (New York: The Lewis Historical Publishing Company, 1913), 2:993-994.

3. Levi and Sarah also lost a child while at Ebenezer, a daughter, who was buried in the church cemetery. *History of Ebenezer Methodist Episcopal Church*, 63, 106-107.

4 "Levi Scott," http://dickinson.edu/.

5. The African Methodist Episcopal (AME) Church was founded in Philadelphia in 1816, in response to racial discrimination within the ME Church. Its founding bishop was Rev. Richard Allen.

6. *Christian Advocate*, February 11, 1846. Tindley Temple became one of largest and most influential black congregations in the nation in the early 20th century. It was renamed for another Delmarva native, Charles Albert Tindley, who gained fame as a preacher and a hymnwriter.

7. John S. J. McConnell, *History of the First Methodist Episcopal Church of the City of Lancaster, PA from 1807 to 1893* (Lancaster: New Era Printing House, 1893), 49, 52-54; and Joseph F. DiPaolo, "*To Your Tents, O Israel!" The Life of Rev. Andrew Manship, Evangelist and Entrepreneur* (Fruitland, MD: Arcadia Enterprises, 2009), 12-14.

8. *Ocean Grove Record*, January 28, 1888. Several women were class leaders when Methodism was still a revival movement, and not yet a church. The first was Mary Thorn, appointed by Joseph Pilmore in 1769 at St. George's, Philadelphia. See George W. Lybrand, "Mary Thorn, First Female Class Leader in American Methodism," in *Annals of Eastern Pennsylvania*, No. 2 (2005), 61-71.

9. For the story of the lawsuit, see James Penn Pilkington, *The Methodist Publishing House: A History, Volume 1; Beginnings to 1870* (Nashville: Abingdon, 1968), 294-326; also, R. Sutton, *The Methodist Property Case: The Report of the Suit of Henry B. Bascom and Others vs. George Lane and Others* (New York: Lane & Scott, 1851).

10. Mitchell, 7-8; Kidder was Sunday school and tract editor in New York, 1848-1852.

11. Sarah Scott to Levi Scott, May 14, 1848; Barratt's Chapel and Museum, Frederica, Delaware.

12. The vote totals are not recorded in the official minutes but may be found in *Fox and Hoyt's Quadrennial Register of the Methodist Episcopal Church and Universal Church Gazetteer* (Hartford, CT: Case, Tiffany & Co., 1852), 130.

13. Mitchell, 150-151.

14. Levi Scott to Sarah Scott, July 24, 1858, Barratt's Chapel and Museum.

15. Mitchell, 179.

16. Mitchell 57-58.

17. Mitchell, 268.

Chapter 4: Bishop Scott and Slavery

1. Matthew Simpson and Edward R. Ames both were from Ohio, and Osman C. Baker was a New Englander.

2. Williams, *Slavery*, 9-10. The transatlantic slave trade, of course, was by this point over a century old, and well established in the Caribbean and South America.

3. After Pennsylvania, states that ended slavery or adopted gradual emancipation were Vermont (1782), Massachusetts (1783), Rhode Island (1784), Connecticut (1784, 1787), New York (1784, 1817), and New Jersey (1804). Williams, *Slavery*, 16-17, 162-163, 180.

4. Williams, *Slavery*, 13, 45-46, 8-89. The inability to sell slaves beyond the border meant that Delaware slave owners could not breed slaves for sale to the states of the deep South, thus reducing their economic value as commodities. Other states, such as Maryland and Virginia did provide slaves for sale across state borders to meet the demand for slave labor in new territories and states, especially after the suspension of the United States' participation in the African Slave trade in 1808, See, Edward E. Baptist, *The Half Has Never Been Told: Slavery and the Making of American Capitalism* (New York: Basic Books, 2014), 1-37.

5. On American Methodism's changing slavery stance, see Donald G. Mathews, *Slavery and Methodism: A Chapter in American Morality, 1780-1845* (Princeton University Press, 1965); see also Gordon Melton, *A Will to Choose: the Origins of African American Methodism* (Lanham, MD: Rowman and Littlefield. 2007), 23-32; Richard K. MacMaster, "Liberty or Property? The Methodists Petition for Emancipation in Virginia, 1785," *Methodist History* 10:3 (October 1971), 44-55.

6. Williams, *Slavery*, 69-70, 150-152. Andrew Barratt was a leading attorney who held various political leadership positions from 1780 to 1820.

7. Kent County Register of Wills, Volume 738, page 140. Sources on Scott's grandparents include Mitchell, 12-15, 24-25; H. Clay Reed., ed., *Delaware, A History of the First State: Personal and Family Records*, Vol III (New York: Lewis Historical Publishing Company, 1947), 58; and *Biographical and Genealogical History*, op. cit., 1232.

8. Williams, *Slavery*, 38-40.

9. Mitchell, 15. A memoir of James Lattomus (1771-1806) appears in 1807, indicating that he joined the Philadelphia Conference in 1796, and ceased traveling for health reasons in 1802. He is described as "a man of feeble habit of body, but some strength of mind and an upright walk." *Minutes of the Annual Conferences of the Methodist Episcopal Church for the Years 1773-1828* (New York: T. Mason and G. Lane, 1840), 107, 112, 146.

10. Jarena Lee, *Religious Experience and Journal of Mrs. Jarena Lee Giving Her Account of Her Call to Preach the Gospel* (Philadelphia: 1849), 27. She was on a Delaware preaching tour that took her through Wilmington,

New Castle, Christiana, Odessa/Canton Bridge (which she calls "Canton Bride") and Smyrna.

11. Joseph F. DiPaolo, ed., *My Business Was to Fight the Devil: Recollections of Rev. Adam Wallace, Peninsula Circuit Rider, 1847-1865* (Acton: Tapestry Press, 1998), 140-142.

12. Henry B. Ridgaway, *The Life of Edmund S. Janes, DD, LLD, Late Senior Bishop of the Methodist Episcopal Church* (New York: Phillips and Hunt, 1882), 85-89.

13. The Snow Hill District, southernmost on the Peninsula and once led by Scott as presiding elder, lost nearly 20% of its white and 18% of its black membership from 1844 to 1850, declining from 9375 whites and 4886 blacks in 1844, to 7573 and 4021, respectively, in 1850; *Philadelphia Conference Minutes* (1844), 3; and (1850), 5. On violence among local Methodists after the split, see Emory Stevens Buck, gen. ed., *The History of American Methodism*, 3 Vols. (Nashville: Abingdon, 1964), 2:162-164. For a short account of the 1844 split, see Robert W. Sledge, "'Till Charity Wept': 1844 Revisited," in *Methodist History* 48:2 (January 2010), 92-112.

14. James Mayland McCarter, *Border Methodism and Border Slavery* (Philadelphia: Collins, 1858), 25-26. On antebellum attitudes within Methodism at large, see Matthews, *Slavery and Methodism*, op. cit.; see also Edward E. Barlow, Jr., *The Philadelphia Annual Conference Attitude Toward the Negro and Slavery in the Years Prior to the Civil War* (Eastern Baptist Theological Seminary: Master of Theology Thesis, 1972).

15. The divide in the Philadelphia Conference is shown by the fact that three of its delegates (Durbin, Scott and Henry White) voted for the resolution, while three (Thomas J. Thompson, Ignatius T. Cooper and William Cooper) voted against it. Mitchell, 63.

16. Durbin published his views in the July 26, 1855 *Christian Advocate*. See John A. Roche, *The Life of John Price Durbin, DD*, 4th ed. (New York: Hunt & Eaton, 1893); and Russell Richey, Kenneth E. Rowe and Jean Miller Schmidt, *The Methodist Experience in Ameri-ca, Volume II: A Sourcebook* (Nashville: Abingdon, 2000), 273-278.

17. Mitchell, 61-62.

18. *Religious Messenger*, March 23, 1826; petition dated March 24, 1861, "Conference Papers," St. George's Church, Philadelphia.

19. Two recent histories of the colonization movement that differ in their assessment are: Eric Burin, *Slavery and the Peculiar Solution: A History of the American Colonization Society* (Gainesville: University Press of Florida, 2005); and Ousamane K. Power-Greene, *Against Wind and Tide: The African American Struggle Against the Colonization Movement* (New York: NYU Press, 2014).

20. Williams, *Slavery*, 167-168, 199-200. Even William Lloyd Garrison, who later denounced the ACS, flirted with the movement in the late 1820s.

21. This first set of colonists, including its leaders, was so decimated by illness that Coker wound up *de facto* governor, and later moved his group to Sierra Leone. Later emigres continued settling territory that became Liberia. Wade Crawford Barclay, *History of Methodist Missions, Vol. 1: Missionary Motivation and Expansion* (New York: Board of Missions and Church Extension of the Methodist Church, 1949), 325-328; Melton, *Will to Choose*, 72-74; and Rhonda R. Thomas, "Exodus and Colonization: Charting the Journey in the Journals of Daniel Coker, A Descendent of Africa," in *African American Review* 41:3 (2007), 507-520.

22. Williams, *Slavery*, 238-239; and Richard Newman, *Freedom's Prophet: Bishop Richard Allen, the AME Church and the Black Founding Fathers* (New York: NYU Press, 2008), 159.

23. *Philadelphia Conference Minutes* (1834), 27-28.

24. James Mitchell (1808-1903) was a native of Northern Ireland; his wife Emma died in 1871. Mitchell took his state papers with him when he left office in 1864, which undoubtedly contained documents in Lincoln's hand; these disappeared after Mitchell's death. See Phillip W. Magness, "James Mitchell and the Mystery of the Emigration Office Papers," *Journal of the Abraham Lincoln Association* 32:2 (September 2011), 50-62; also Philip W. Magness and Sebastian N. Page, *Colonization after Emancipation: Lincoln and the Movement for Black Resettlement* (Columbia: University of Missouri Press, 2011); and *Georgia Conference Minutes* (1904), 30.

25. Mitchell, 247.

Chapter 5: Trip to Liberia

1. On the history of the Liberian Mission, see Barclay, op. cit., I:325-344, and Wade Crawford Barclay, *History of Methodist Missions, Vol. 3: Widening Horizons* (New York: Board of Missions of the Methodist Church, 1957), 869-880; on Melville Cox, see Gershom F. Cox, ed., *Remains of Melville B. Cox, Late Missionary to Liberia: With a Memoir* (Boston: Light and Horton, 1835). Cox was famous for saying, "Let a thousand fall before Africa be given up!"

2. Handwritten account by Bishop Waugh, Lovely Lane Museum, Baltimore. The quote from St. Paul is from Acts 20:24.

3. Mitchell, 89-90. Much of Bishop Scott's journal is transcribed and included verbatim in Mitchell's biography, covering 80 of its 272 pages. An 1853 date book with notes, which probably was used by Scott as a basis for his journal narrative, as well as a portion of the original handwritten journal itself which Mitchell transcribed, are in the collection at Barratt's Chapel and Museum.

4. "Remarks of Bishop Scott," *African Repository*, Vol. XXX (Washington: C. Alexander, 1854), 180.

5. "Remarks of Bishop Scott," 181.

6. Barclay, 3:877-878.

7. The 1853 Liberia Conference session is covered in Mitchell, 135-139; see also *Journals of the Liberia Annual Conference, ME Church, 1851-1853* (Typescript copy at GCAH, Madison, New Jersey), 15-29. The latter includes a transcript of Bishop Scott's opening address of March 7, printed here as Appendix C, pages 121-126.

8. Scott first quotes from Revelation 20:13, then from a hymn by Isaac Watts, "And Must This Body Die?"

9. Mitchell, 140-149 contains Scott's journal of his return voyage. He also was given a parrot. It is not clear what Bishop Scott did with either the monkey or the parrot after returning to America.

10. Barclay, 3:878.

11. "Remarks of Bishop Scott," 180-182.

12. Mitchell, 105. Excerpts of Scott's report to the Society may be found in *Thirty-Fifth Annual Report of the Missionary Society of the Methodist Episcopal Church* (New York: 1854), 105-110.

13. Barclay, 3:880-881; James M. Buckley, *Constitutional and Parliamentary History of the Methodist Episcopal Church* (New York: Eaton & Mains, 1912), 222-227; and William R. Phinney, *From Chore Boy to Bishop: The Story of Francis Burns, First Missionary Bishop of the Methodist Episcopal Church* (New York: Commission on Archives and History, 1970).

14. *Journals of the General Conferences of the Methodist Episcopal Church, Vol. III: 1848-1856* (New York: Carlton and Porter, 1856), 1848: 35, 130 and 1852:65; and *Minutes of the Convention of Colored Pastors of the Methodist Episcopal Church Convened in Zoar Church, Philadelphia* (1852), reprinted in Lewis Y. Cox, *Pioneer Footsteps* (Cape May, NJ: Star and Wave Press, 1917), 5-10.

15. *The Journals of Dr. Thomas Coke*, ed. John A. Vickers (Nashville: Kingswood Books, 2005), 37. On "Black Harry" Hosier, see Warren Thomas Smith, *Harry Hosier, Circuit Rider* (Nashville: The Upper Room, 1981).

16. *Journals of the General Conferences*, op. cit., 1856:183.

17. *Christian Advocate*, August 13, 1857.

18. *Minutes of the Delaware Conference of the Methodist Episcopal Church, 1877-1882* (Bound, handwritten volume, in the possession of Zoar United Methodist Church, Philadelphia).

Chapter 6: War Bishop

1. Levi Scott to Henry Slicer, January 10, 1861, F. D. Leete Collection. Rev. Henry Slicer (1801-1874), was a leading member of the Baltimore Conference, who served several terms as a presiding elder, and as Chaplain of the US Senate.

2. *Doctrines and Discipline of the Methodist Episcopal Church* (1860), 266.

3. Levi Scott, "The New Chapter," in *Christian Advocate*, May 9, 1861; italics original.

4. *Christian Advocate*, April 4, 1861. For an account of church secessions on the Virginia shore, see Kirk Mariner, *Revival's Children: A Religious History of Virginia's Eastern Shore* (Salisbury, MD: Peninsula Press, 1979), 115-121.

5. S. V. Leech, "Bishop Scott's Memorable Conference at Staunton, Virginia," in *Christian Advocate*, July 29, 1886; *Baltimore Conference Minutes* (1861), 5-9; and "Proceedings of the Baltimore Conference," in *Christian Advocate*, March 21, 28 and April 4, 1861. For an account of the Baltimore Conference secession movement, see Homer L. Clakin, "The Slavery Struggle, 1780-1865," in *Those Incredible Methodists: A History of the Baltimore Conference of the United Methodist Church*, ed., Gordon Pratt Baker (Baltimore: Commission on Archives and History, 1972), 218-224.

6. *Baltimore Conference Minutes* (1861), 21.

7. Ibid., 22; and William Warren Sweet, *The Methodist Episcopal Church and the Civil War* (Cincinnati: Methodist Book Concern, 1912), 49.

8. Levi Scott to Henry Slicer, April 1, 1861, Lovely Lane Museum.

9. Levi Scott to Henry Slicer, May 24, 1861, F. D. Leete Collection; and Mitchell, 168.

10. Cornelia Scott to Levi Scott, April 29, 1861. Barratt's Chapel Museum and Library.

11. Simpson is quoted in James E. Kirby, "The McKendree Chapel Affair" in *Tennessee Historical Quarterly* 25:4 (Winter 1966), 360. On the story of the MEC's mission to the South, see Barclay, 3:299-324; and Bucke, *History of American Methodism*, 2:247-251.

12. Barclay, 3:302, and Kirby, 361-362.

13. Levi Scott to Matthew Simpson, March 10, 1864, Matthew Simpson Papers, St. George's Church, Philadelphia.

14. Barclay, 304.

15. The conference was formally organized January 3, 1867; Mitchell, 175, 218-219.

16. Barclay, 3:309.

17. *Journal of the General Conference of the Methodist Episcopal Church, Held in Philadelphia, Pa., 1864* (New York: Carlton & Porter, 1864), 167, 217, 224, 440, 487.

18. Lewis W. Baldwin, "The Convention of Colored Local Preachers: Forerunner of the Delaware Annual Conference," in *Commemorative Booklet: Delaware Annual Conference, 1864-1965* (Dover: Peninsula Conference Commission on Archives and History, 1990), 10-15; *Delaware Conference Minutes* (1864); David W. Brown, *Freedom from Within: A History of the Delaware Annual Conference of the United Methodist Church* ([Philadelphia]: 2010).

19. Levi Scott to N. J. B. Morgan, July 30, 1864, Lovely Lane Museum and Library.

20. *Washington Conference Minutes* (1864), 9.

21. Ibid, 8-9.

22. Ibid.

23. William B. Gravely, *Gilbert Haven, Methodist Abolitionist* (Nashville: Abingdon, 1973), 129-132.

24. In the years after the Civil War, the mission conferences established in the South were systematically divided by race, a process that was completed by 1895, at which time the more than 226,000 black members of the ME Church were entirely organized into segregated conferences. Barclay, 3:314-321.

Chapter 7: Senior Bishop

1. Mitchell, 182-183. Bishops Edward Thomson and Calvin Kingsley died in 1870; 1871 saw the passing of Davis W. Clark and Osman C. Baker (Baker had been on limited duty since suffering debilitating illness in 1866). In addition, Bishop Thomas Morris had retired due to poor health in 1864.

2. Mitchell, 182.

3. Levi Scott to Matthew Simpson, February 22, 1867, Matthew Simpson Papers, St. George's.

4. In the 1890s the school was renamed for Rev. Lyttleton F. Morgan, first trustee chair and land donor. In 1939, the school was purchased by the state as a public college. In 1887 a branch of the school was established in Princess Anne and is today's University of Maryland Eastern Shore. See Edward N. Wilson, *The History of Morgan State College: A Century of Purpose in Action, 1867-1967* (New York: Vantage Press, 1975). Scott returned in June 1880 to help lead the cornerstone laying ceremony for the first building erected by the school. *Baltimore Sun*, June 17, 1880.

5. *Delaware Conference Minutes* (1879), 4; and Lewis Y. Cox, *Pioneer Footsteps*, 68-69. An account of the 1879 session and a tribute to Bishop Scott appear in William C. Jason, Jr. *A Methodist Trail: Through Slavery and Racism Before, During and Since the Colored Local Preachers and Delaware Annual Conference of the Methodist Episcopal and Methodist Church*, 2 vols. ([Philadelphia]: William Jason, Jr., 2014), 1:108-113, 297-308. Of Bishop Scott, Jason says, "If ever a man was allowed to see for himself the result he had fought to set men free, Levi Scott was that man. May he know all the while that in the memories of the Delaware Conference, his place is fixed."

6. Ibid., 32.

7. Levi Scott, "Semi-Centennial Sermon," 73-80.

8. Levi Scott to Matthew Simpson, December 6, 1877, Matthew Simpson Papers, St. George's Church, Philadelphia.

9. Mitchell, 191-239, relates in detail his travels with Bishop Scott in 1878. Dates and places of each conference are in *Minutes of the Annual Conferences for 1878* (New York: Philips and Hunt, 1879).

10. Mitchell, 207, 230-231.

11. Mitchell, 231, 237-238.

12. Bucke, *History of American Methodism*, 2:456; *Chicago Tribune*, May 12, 1870; and Mitchell, 208, 211-213.

13. *Wilmington Conference Minutes* (1880), 48.

14. Levi Scott to James Mitchell, quoted in Mitchell, 244.

15. Levi Scott to Matthew Simpson, April 13, 1880, Matthew Simpson Papers, St. George's Church, Philadelphia.

16. Quoted in "Bishop Scott," in *Christian Advocate*, July 20, 1882.

17. *New York Times*, November 6, 1880. Many of Scott's extant letters from the 1870s and 1880s are written on stationary headed with the words, "Itinerants Lodge, Odessa, Del."

18. *Christian Advocate*, December 2, 1880.

19. "Bishop Levi Scott," in *Journal of the General Conference* (1884), 513-514.

20. Robert W. Todd, *Methodism of the Peninsula* (Philadelphia: ME Book Room, 1886), 263-267.

21. *Wilmington Conference Minutes* (1883), 466.

22. Mitchell, 260-261.

23. *New York Times*, July 14, 1882.

24. *Philadelphia Methodist*, July 20, 1882.

25. *Minutes of the Delaware Conference of the Methodist Episcopal Church, 1877-1882* (Bound, handwritten volume, in possession of Zoar United Methodist Church, Philadelphia), 196-197.

Sources

The primary source for Scott's life is James Mitchell, *The Life and Times of Levi Scott, DD* (New York: Phillips and Hunt, 1885). Mitchell, Scott's son-in-law, had access to the bishop's personal papers, much of which has disappeared, including an 1859 autobiographical sketch found on pages 24-38. Sketches of Scott include: J. A. Roche, "Bishop Levi Scott," in *Methodist Review* 68:2 (July 1886), 489-511; "Bishop" Scott," in *Christian Advocate* (New York), July 20, 1882; J. B. McCullough, "Death of Bishop Scott," in *Philadelphia Methodist* (July 20, 1882); "Bishop Levi Scott" in *Wilmington Conference Minutes* (1883), 45-46; "Bishop Levi Scott," in *Journal of the General Conference of the Methodist Episcopal Church* (New York: Phillips and Hunt, 1884), 510-515; and "Levi Scott," in *Biographical and Genealogical History of the State of Delaware* (Chambersburg: J. M. Runk and Co., 1899), 1232-1234. A collection of Scott's letters are in the F. D. Leete Collection on Methodist Bishops, Bridwell Library, Southern Methodist University (Dallas, Texas). Another collection of papers, including an 1853 journal, and a book of sermon briefs, are in the collection at Barratt's Chapel and Museum (Frederica, Delaware). Other letters of Scott are scattered among papers in the archives of St. George's (Philadelphia), The General Commission on Archives and History (Madison, New Jersey), Lovely Lane Museum and Library (Baltimore), Boston University School of Theology Archive (Boston), and Wilmington (Delaware) Historical Society.

Baker, Gordon Pratt, ed. *Those Incredible Methodists: A History of the Baltimore Conference of the United Methodist Church.* Baltimore: Commission on Archives and History, 1972.

Baptist, Edward E. *The Half Has Never Been Told: Slavery and the Making of American Capitalism.* New York: Basic Books, 2014.

Barclay, Wade Crawford. *History of Methodist Missions.* 6 vols. New York: Board of Missions and Church Extension Society of the Methodist Church, 1949.

Barlow, Edward E., Jr. *The Philadelphia Annual Conference Attitude Toward the Negro and Slavery in the Years Prior to the Civil War.* Eastern Baptist Theological Seminary: Master of Theology Thesis, 1972.

Biographical and Genealogical History of the State of Delaware. 2 vols. Chambersburg: J. M. Runk & Co., 1899.

Bonner, Hannah, "Abolitionist on Trial: Rev. John D. Long and the 1858 Philadelphia Conference," in *Annals of Eastern Pennsylvania* No. 5, (2008), 3-25.

Brown, David W. "Chasing Steeples: African Americans in the United Methodist Church." *Annals of Eastern Pennsylvania,* No. 6 (2009), 45-63.

Brown, David W. *Freedom From Within: A History of the Delaware Annual Conference of the United Methodist Church.* [Philadelphia]: 2010.

Bucke, Emory Stevens, et. al. *The History of American Methodism.* 3 vols. Nashville: Abingdon, 1964.

Buckley, James M. *Constitutional and Parliamentary History of the Methodist Episcopal Church.* New York: Eaton and Mains, 1912.

Burin, Erin. *Slavery and the Peculiar Solution: A History of the American Colonization Society.* Gainesville: University Press of Florida, 2005.

Caley, George L. *A History of Asbury United Methodist Church, Smyrna, Delaware, Founded 1778.* Smyrna: Shane Quality Press, 1972.

Campbell, Ted A. "'The Way of Salvation' and the Methodist Ethos Beyond John Wesley: A Study in Formal Consensus and Popular Reception." *Asbury Journal* 65:1 (2008), 5-31.

"Centenary of Bishop Levi Scott." *Christian Advocate,* October 9, 1902.

Clark, Elmer S., ed. *The Journal and Letters of Francis Asbury.* 3 vols. Nashville: Abingdon, 1958.

Clark, Robert D. *The Life of Bishop Matthew Simpson.* New York: Macmillan, 1956.

Collins, Kenneth, and John H. Tyson. *Conversion in the Wesleyan Tradition.* Abingdon: Nashville, 2001.

Commemorative Booklet: Delaware Annual Conference, 1864-1965. Dover: Peninsula Conference Commission on Archives and History, 1990.

Cox, Gershom F., ed., *Remains of Melville B. Cox, Late Missionary to Liberia: With a Memoir.* Boston: Light and Horton, 1835.

Cox, Lewis Y. *Pioneer Footsteps.* Cape May, New Jersey: Star and Wave Press, 1917.

Crooks, George R. *The Life of Bishop Matthew Simpson of the Methodist Episcopal Church.* New York: Harper and Brothers, 1891.

Cutter, William R., gen. ed. *American Biography: A New Cyclopedia, Vol. VI.* New York: The American Historical Society, 1919.

DiPaolo, Joseph F., ed. *My Business Was to Fight the Devil: Recollections of Rev. Adam Wallace, Peninsula Circuit Rider, 1847-1865.* Acton, MA: Tapestry Press, 1998.

DiPaolo, Joseph F. "So Shall Their Chains Fall Off": Bishop Levi Scott and Nineteenth-Century Black Methodism. *Methodist History* 55:4 (July 2017), 241-264.

DiPaolo, Joseph F. *"To Your Tents, O Israel!" The Life of Rev. Andrew Manship, Evangelist and Entrepreneur.* Fruitland, MD: Arcadia Enterprises, 2009.

Duffin, Barbara and Philip Lawton. *Cultivating the Methodist Garden: A Brief History of the Peninsula-Delaware Conference of the United Methodist Church.* Frederica: Barratt's Chapel Museum, 2000.

Ferguson, Charles. *Organizing to Beat the Devil; Methodists and the Making of America.* Garden City, New York: Doubleday, 1971.

Flood, Theodore L. and John Hamilton. *Lives of Methodist Bishops.* New York, Phillips and Hunt; 1882.

"Founding of the Delaware Conference: An Eyewitness Account." *Annals of Eastern Pennsylvania,* No. 2 (2005), 37-42.

Fox and Hoyt's Quadrennial Register of the Methodist Episcopal Church and Universal Church Gazetteer. Hartford: Case, Tiffany & Co., 1852.

Gravely, William B. *Gilbert Haven, Methodist Abolitionist.* Nashville: Abingdon, 1973.

Guyatt, Nicholas. "'The Outskirts of Our Happiness:' Race and the Lure of Colonization in the Early Republic." *Journal of American History* 95:4 (March 2009), 986-1011.

Hall, Amy Laura. *Conceiving Parenthood: American Protestantism and the Spirit of Reproduction.* Grand Rapids: Eerdmans, 2008.

Hallman, E. C. *The Garden of Methodism.* Peninsula Annual Conference, 1948.

Hatch, Nathan O., and John Wigger, eds. *Methodism and the Shaping of American Culture.* Nashville: Kingswood Books, 2001.

Hempton, David. *Methodism: Empire of the Spirit.* New Haven: Yale University Press, 2005.

History of Ebenezer Methodist Episcopal Church of Southwark, Philadelphia. Philadelphia: J. B. Lippincott Company, 1890.

Jason, William C., Jr. *A Methodist Trail: Through Slavery and Racism Before, During and Since the Colored Local Preachers and Delaware Annual Conference of the Methodist Episcopal and Methodist Church.* 2 vols. [Philadelphia]: William Jason, Jr., 2014.

Journal of the General Conference of the Methodist Episcopal Church, Held in Philadelphia, Pa., 1864. New York: Carlton and Porter, 1864.

Journal of the General Conference of the Methodist Episcopal Church, Held in Philadelphia, May 1-28, 1884. New York: Phillips and Hunt, 1884.

Journals of the General Conferences of the Methodist Episcopal Church, Vol. I: 1796-1836. New York: Carlton and Phillips, 1855.

Journals of the General Conferences of the Methodist Episcopal Church, Vol. II: 1840, 1844, Together with the Debates of 1844. New York: Carlton and Phillips, 1856.

Journals of the General Conferences of the Methodist Episcopal Church, Vol. III: 1848-1856. New York: Carlton and Porter, 1856.

Kirby, James E. *The Episcopacy in American Methodism*. Nashville: Kingswood Books, 2000.

Kirby, James E. "The McKendree Chapel Affair." *Tennessee Historical Quarterly* 25:4 (Winter 1966), 360-370.

Kisker, Scott. "Methodist Abroad: Matthew Simpson and the Emergence of American Methodism as a World Church." *Methodist History* 53:1 (October 2014), 4-20.

Koch, Harold. *The Leaven of the Kingdom: The Amazing Growth of Methodism in the Philadelphia Conference, 1767-1968*. Ephrata: Science Press, 1983.

Lednum, John. *A History of the Rise of Methodism in America*. Philadelphia: By the Author, 1859.

Lee, Jarena. *Religious Experience and Journal of Mrs. Jarena Lee, Giving Her Account of Her Call to Preach the Gospel*. Philadelphia: For the Author, 1849.

Leete, Frederick D. *Methodist Bishops: Personal Notes and Bibliography*. Nashville: The Parthenon Press, 1948.

Longenecker, Stephen L. *Shenandoah Religion: Outsiders and the Mainstream, 1716-1865*. Waco: Baylor University Press, 2002

Lore, Charles D. *History of Odessa; Address of Chief Justice Lore at the Methodist Episcopal Church, November 18, 1901*.

MacMaster, Richard K. "Liberty or Property? The Methodists Petition for Emancipation in Virginia, 1785." *Methodist History* 10:3 (October 1971), 44-55.

McCarter, James Mayland. *Border Methodism and Border Slavery*. Philadelphia: Collins, 1858.

McConnell, John S. J. *History of the First Methodist Episcopal Church of the of Lancaster, PA from 1807 to 1893*. Lancaster: New Era Printing House, 1893.

McDonald, William and John Searles. *The Life of Rev. John S. Inskip*. Boston: McDonald and Gill, 1885.

McKivigan, John R. and Mitchell Snay, eds. *Religion and the Antebellum Debate over Slavery*. Athens: University of Georgia Press, 1998.

Magness, Phillip W. "James Mitchell and the Mystery of the Emigration Office Papers." *Journal of the Abraham Lincoln Association* 32:2 (September 2011), 50-62.

Magness, Phillip W. and Sebastian N. Page, *Colonization after Emancipation Lincoln and the Movement for Black Resettlement.* Columbia: University of Missouri Press, 2011.

Marclay, John F. *The Life of Rev. Thomas S. Morris, DD, Late Senior Bishop of the Methodist Episcopal Church.* Cincinnati: Hitchcock and Walden, 1875.

Mariner, Kirk. *Revival's Children: A Religious History of Virginia's Eastern Shore.* Salisbury: Peninsula Press, 1979.

Mathews, Donald G. *Slavery and Methodism: A Chapter in American Morality, 1780-1845.* Princeton University Press, 1965.

Melton, J. Gordon. *A Will to Choose: The Origins of African American Methodism.* Lanham, MD: Rowman and Littlefield. 2007.

Memorials of the Semi-Centennial of St. Paul's ME Church, Odessa, Delaware, 1833-1883. Wilmington: The Conference Worker Print, 1883.

Mills, Brandon. "'The United States of Africa:' Liberian Independence and the Contested Meaning of a Black Republic." *Journal of the Early American Republic* 34 (Spring 2014), 79-108.

Minutes of the Annual Conferences of the Methodist Episcopal Church for the Years 1773-1828. New York: T. Mason and G. Lane, 1840.

Mitchell, James. *The Life and Times of Levi Scott, DD.* New York: Phillips and Hunt, 1885.

Moses, Wilson J. *Liberian Dreams: Back-to-Africa Narratives from the 1850s.* University Park: Penn State University Press, 1998.

Napheys, George H. *The Transmission of Life.* Philadelphia: J. Fergus, 1871.

Newman, Richard. *Freedom's Prophet: Bishop Richard Allen, the AME Church and the Black Founding Fathers.* New York: NYU Press, 2008.

Noll, Mark A. *The Civil War as a Theological Crisis.* Chapel Hill: University of North Carolina Press, 2006.

Norwood, Frederick A. *The Story of American Methodism.* Nashville: Abingdon, 1974.

Painter, Kyle. "The Pro-Slavery Argument in the Development of the American Methodist Church," *Constructing the Past.* 2:1 the (2001), 29-46. Available online at http://digitalcommons. iwu.edu/constructing/vol2/iss1/5.

Phinney, William R. *From Chore Boy to Bishop: The Story of Francis Burns, First Missionary Bishop of the Methodist Episcopal Church.* New York: Commission on Archives and History, 1970.

Phoebus, George A. *Beams of Light on Early Methodism in America. Chiefly Drawn from the Diary, Letters, Manuscripts, Documents, and Original Tracts of the Rev. Ezekiel Cooper.* New York: Phillips and Hunt, 1887.

Pilkington, James Penn. *The Methodist Publishing House: A History, Vol. 1; Beginnings to 1870* (Nashville: Abingdon, 1968), 229-258.

Polgar, Paul J. "'To Raise Them to an Equal Participation:' Early National Abolitionism, Gradual Emancipation, and the Promise of African American Citizenship." *Journal of the Early Republic* 31 (Summer 2011), 229-258.

Power-Greene, Ousamane K. *Against Wind and Tide: The African American Struggle Against the Colonization Movement.* New York: NYU Press, 2014.

Pryor, Clifford. *The Forest of Appoquinimink.* Milford: Shawnee Printing, 1975.

Reed, H. Clay, ed. *Delaware: A History of the First State.* 3 vols. New York Lewis Historical Publishing Company, 1947.

Richey, Russell, Kenneth E. Rowe, and Jean Miller Schmidt. *The Methodist Experience in America, Volume I: A History.* Nashville: Abingdon, 2010.

Richey, Russell, Kenneth E. Rowe, and Jean Miller Schmidt. *The Methodist Experience in America, Volume II: A Sourcebook.* Nashville: Abingdon, 2000.

Ridgaway, Henry B. *The Life of Edmund S. Janes, DD, LLD, Late Senior Bishop of the Methodist Episcopal Church.* New York: Phillips and Hunt, 1882.

Roche, John A. *Autobiography and Sermons, Together with the Expressions Elicited by his Death.* New York: Eaton and Mains, [1898].

Roche, John A. "Bishop Levi Scott." *Methodist Review* 68:2 (July 1886), 489-511.

Roche, John A. *The Life of John Price Durbin, DD, LLD, with an Analysis of his Homiletical Skill and Sacred Oratory.* New York: Hunt and Eaton, 1893.

Rose, Eric. *The Charleston "School of Slavery:" Race, Religion and Community in the Capital of Southern Civilization.* (Doctoral dissertation, 2014). Online at http://scholarcommons.sc.edu/etd/2763.

Ruth, Lester. *A Little Heaven Below: Worship at Early Methodist Quarterly Meetings.* Nashville: Kingswood Books, 2000.

Scott, Levi. "Semi-Centennial Sermon." *Wilmington Conference Minutes* (1876), 73-80.

Sharp, L. Corwin. *The Janvier Family of Odessa, Delaware.* MA Thesis, University of Delaware, 1980.

Sledge, Robert W. "'Till Charity Wept': 1844 Revisited," *Methodist History* 48:2 (January 2010), 92-112.

Stowell, Daniel W. *Rebuilding Zion: The Religious Reconstruction of the South, 1863-1877.* New York: Oxford, 1998.

Strickland, William P. *The Life of Jacob Gruber.* New York: Carlton and Porter, 1860.

Sutton, R. *The Methodist Property Case: The Report of the Suit of Henry B. Bascom and Others vs. George Lane and Others.* New York: Lane and Scott, 1851.

Sweet, William Warren. *Methodism in American History*. rev. ed. Nashville: Abingdon, 1953.

Sweet, William Warren. *The Methodist Episcopal Church and the Civil War*. Cincinnati: Methodist Book Concern, 1912.

Teasdale, Mark R. "Evangelism and Identity in Early American Methodism." *Wesleyan Theological Journal* 47:2 (Fall 2012), 89-109.

Tees, Francis H., et al. *Pioneering in Penn's Woods: Philadelphia Methodist Episcopal Annual Conference Through One Hundred Fifty Years*. Philadelphia: Philadelphia Conference Historical Society, 1937.

The Centennial Services of Asbury Methodist Episcopal Church, Wilmington, Delaware. Wilmington: Delaware Printing Company, 1889.

Thirty-Fifth Annual Report of the Missionary Society of the Methodist Episcopal Church. New York: 1854.

Thomas, Rhonda R. "Exodus and Colonization: Charting the Journey in the Journals of Daniel Coker, A Descendent of Africa." *African American Review* 41:3 (2007), 507-520.

Todd, Robert W. *Methodism of the Peninsula*. Philadelphia: Methodist Book Room, 1886.

Urquhart, Frank John. *A History of the City of Newark, New Jersey*. 2 vols. New York: The Lewis Historical Publishing Company, 1913.

Vickers, John A., ed. *The Journals of Dr. Thomas Coke*. Nashville: Kingswood Books, 2005.

Wallace, Adam. *The Parson of the Islands*. Philadelphia, 1861.

Ware, Thomas. *Sketches of the Life and Travels of Rev. Thomas Ware*. New York: Mason and Land, 1839.

Wheeler, Marcia Rae. *That Old Bat Church*. Wilmington: Cedar Tree Books, 2015.

Wigger, John. *American Saint: Francis Asbury and the Methodists*. New York: Oxford University Press, 2009.

Wigger, John. *Taking Heaven by Storm: Methodism and the Rise of Popular Christianity in America*. New York: Oxford University Press, 1998.

Williams, William H. *Slavery and Freedom in Delaware, 1639-1865*. Wilmington: Scholarly Resources, 1996.

Williams, William H. *The Garden of American Methodism: The Delmarva Peninsula, 1769-1820*. Wilmington: The Peninsula Conference, 1984.

Wilson, Edward N. *The History of Morgan State College: A Century of Purpose in Action, 1867-1967*. New York: Vantage Press, 1975.

Zebley, Frank R. *The Churches of Delaware: A History, in Brief, of the Nearly 900 Churches and Former Churches in Delaware as Located by the Author*. Wilmington: William N. Cann, Inc., 1947.

Index